Slim Moore, Alaska Master Guide

Slim Moore, at Summit Lake Lodge, December, 1956. JIM REARDEN

Slim Moore, Alaska Master Guide

*A Sourdough's Hunting
Adventures and Wisdom*

by JIM REARDEN

PICTORIAL HISTORIES PUBLISHING COMPANY
Missoula, Montana

Copyright © 2008 by Jim Rearden
All rights reserved.

Library of Congress
Control Number 2008923445

ISBN 978-1-57510-139-2

First Printing: March 2008

Design and composition by Arrow Graphics
www.arrowgraphics.org

Printed by Friesens, Altona, Manitoba, Canada

COVER PHOTO: Slim Moore with the record-holding Brennan-Johnson Dall ram where it fell. Johnson River country, Alaska Range, 1950 (see chapter 11).

Published by Pictorial Histories Publishing Company, Inc.
713 South Third Street West, Missoula, Montana 59801
PHONE (406) 549-8488, FAX (406) 728-9280
EMAIL phpc@montana.com
www.pictorialhistoriespublishing.com

Contents

Foreword, by Alaska Governor Sarah Palin   *vi*
Acknowledgments   *ix*
Introduction   *xi*
1. When Hollywood Came to Alaska   *1*
2. M. W. (Slim) Moore   *16*
3. Riding a Ram Down a Mountain   *24*
4. Chasing Moose   *36*
5. Chasing Griz Over a Mountain   *45*
6. A Bare-handed Encounter with a Wolf   *53*
7. The Parbuckled Brownie, and other Bear Oddities   *62*
8. Close Encounters with Interior Grizzlies   *72*
9. The Midnight Charge of a Brown Bear   *80*
10. One-shot Bill, a Trophy Bull, and the Ways of Moose   *88*
11. The Johnson-Brennan Record Ram   *103*
12. Woes of a Guide   *114*
13. Stalking Sheep, and Memories of Early Days   *130*

Foreword

AUTHOR JIM REARDEN embodies all that is great about Alaska, and for me, that means he embodies what is best about America. A true original, he has not only told some of the best stories about our state and its people, he has played an important role in making Alaska what it is.

Alaska's first inhabitants called this place "The Great Land," and today more than ever this state provides a stunning expression of the grandeur that the natural world has to offer. The state was founded almost fifty years ago by people, who, like Jim, loved the mountains, the rivers, the flora and the fauna of this remarkable place with a deep devotion, and had a commitment to responsible stewardship of our fish and wildlife.

This sense of stewardship has always guided Alaska's fish and game management. And as an educator of wildlife biologists in the state, and a long-time member of the Board of Fish and Game and Board of Game, Jim Rearden has helped embed this ethic in our people and our process.

The wise people who wrote Alaska's Constitution insisted that our fish and wildlife be maintained on the sustained yield principle. This requirement, unique among constitutions everywhere, as implemented by generations of dedicated public servants like Jim, has been instrumental in the growth of our world-renowned fisheries, and the hunting and wildlife opportunities that make Alaska the place where dreams come true.

Throughout his long and impressive career, Jim has had an appreciation for those who came before him. He told me that he recently re-read the transcript of tape-recorded conversations he had more that fifty years ago with his friend Slim Moore, a significant figure in the early history of hunting and guiding in Alaska, and the subject of this book. Immediately appreciating the historical value of the stories Slim had told him all those years ago, and knowing well the joy of telling a good yarn, Jim decided to gather them for this book.

I was deeply honored when he asked me to write this brief foreword, following as I do in this and in so many things, the footsteps of the late Governor Jay Hammond, whose office I am humbled to occupy.

Jay valued the role that our hunting heritage has played in the Alaskan mindset, and he took seriously his responsibility to respect the ethics of hunting and guiding. The great guides and hunters of Alaska—the best place to hunt on earth—show appropriate respect to their prey, and to all the animals as well as to the natural environment that nurtures them. In this book Jim Rearden tells the story of a man who understood this implicitly, and who is a fine example of the hard working, ethical spirit of stewardship that have given us the Alaska we know—where men, women and children hunt, fish and enjoy the most beautiful, wild Great Land anywhere. All of us who are blessed to live here are in their debt.

— Sarah Palin
Governor of Alaska

Acknowledgments

I VERY MUCH APPRECIATE the graceful foreword that Governor Sarah Palin took time from her busy schedule to write for this volume. Clearly, she has a deep understanding of, and a broad perspective on, the wonders and values of Alaska's rich renewable natural resources. That perspective, in my view, was lacking from some former administrations. Slim Moore, subject of this book, would have agreed with her every word on that subject, as do I.

Thanks, Governor Palin. Your words sing. You may have overdone your praise for me, but I'll accept it anyway.

Thanks are also owed to Rosemarie Olsen, Slim Moore's daughter, who, for use in this book, loaned me all of the photos she had of her father, and helped me with biographical information on Slim.

Thanks too, to Darrell Farmen, who thought enough of Slim to include Morris (Slim's seldom-heard first name) as one of his son Kristjan's names, and who obligingly wrote the message about Slim's stories that appears on the front cover.

My thanks also go to Sterling Eide, retired wildlife biologist of the Alaska Department of Fish and Game, with whom I worked on many a wildlife issue as a member of the Board of Game. He contributed the message about Slim Moore that appears on the back cover.

Introduction

THE HUNTING STORIES AND WILDERNESS WISDOM of Slim Moore found in this volume are a distillation of tape-recorded interviews I had with Moore in December, 1956. Where feasible, I have used Slim's words.

Shortly after my visit with Slim, I transcribed the tapes, and during ensuing years I wrote several magazine articles based on the material. In early 2007, while perusing the 60,000-word transcript I realized it had a certain historic value, that Slim Moore and his experiences formed an interesting link with the guided hunting culture of early 20th century Alaska. I then organized it into the present 46,000 word presentation.

I first met this six-foot-three, 200-pound, silver-haired, jut-jawed pioneering guide in the summer of 1950. He was big physically, and, over the next thirty-two years of our friendship, I learned he was also big in spirit, actions, and principle. No one ever called him anything but "Slim." A fellow pioneer who had known him forty years, and eulogized him at his funeral, admitted he didn't know Slim's given name until the day after he died.

I had arrived at Fairbanks that summer, having been hired to organize a new Department of Wildlife Management at the University of Alaska. That day we were both at the Tanana Valley Sportsman's clubhouse on the bank of the Chena River. As Slim told his stories, half a dozen admiring and respectful members of the Tanana Valley Sportsman's Club gathered around him to listen.

Fresh from the University of Maine, with a still-wet Master's Degree in Wildlife Conservation, I was awed by his stories of grizzly bears, Dall sheep, moose, and his life in wilderness Alaska. When we were introduced, Moore said in his courteous way, his blue eyes serious, "Alaska needs to train its own wildlife biologist. We're glad you're here."

Slim Moore was more than a guide. He was a conservationist whose main interest in life was the welfare of Alaska's fish and game. Territorial and State wildlife officials often consulted with Slim on wildlife issues. His opinions were highly valued.

Slim was a great story teller, a raconteur who could make you laugh, cry, or keep you on the edge of your chair. He had an encyclopedic knowledge of the habits of Alaska's big game, which came from living with them. He knew how to make his stories about them interesting.

I resigned my professorship at the University in 1954 to make a living as a writer. At the time, I asked Slim if I could visit him with a tape recorder and capture some of his stories and knowledge of Alaska's wildlife. To this he readily agreed. It took me a year and a half to get around to that visit. I spent five days with Slim and his wife Margaret, and they treated me as an honored guest.

It was 30 degrees below zero on December 14, 1956, when I arrived at their above-timberline lodge at Summit Lake. As I pulled off the gravel Richardson Highway and parked at the lodge, a cross fox that had been snooping around the buildings, trotted off across frozen Summit Lake.

The neat and clean lodge, on the edge of the lake, consisted of the joined original two log cabins Slim had built, a small diner, five oil-stove-heated cabins, and gas pumps. For electricity, a diesel-powered Witte generator ran twenty-four hours a day. Slim had devised a way of scavenging heat from the Witte to warm his living quarters (the original log cabins). Exhaust from the generator was carried some distance, and its thud-thud-thudding was aimed at the lake; it could scarcely be heard inside the building.

In those years it wasn't unusual for the Richardson Highway to be closed for days by great blizzards. Summit Lake Lodge was an oasis on such occasions—a life-saving refuge for travelers.

Summit Lake Lodge, on the shore of Summit Lake, Alaska Range, 1956. Richardson Highway in foreground. JIM REARDEN

"I prefer winters here," Slim told me. "There's not much traffic, and I feel like I own the whole country then." Only three cars had stopped during the previous four days before I arrived.

With his horses, in his early years Slim occasionally made solo exploratory trips. He told me, "I hardly had two dimes to rub together, and my clothing was mostly rags, but I felt rich when I sat on a hillside in the Maclaren River country, and as far as I could see there were moose, caribou, and bears. I wouldn't have changed places with anyone anywhere. I felt as if I owned the whole country."

He remembered the time when he and two other men were mining for gold high in the Alaska Range, and they ran out of all food but moose meat. "We made what we called moose sandwiches; two well-cooked slabs of moose meat, one on each side of a rare middle piece."

Slim firmly believed in fair chase while hunting. When I interviewed him, aerial polar bear hunting was becoming popular and legal along the arctic coast of Alaska; guides with small planes flew over the sea ice with clients, and landed near the bears to allow the hunters to stalk and shoot them.

Slim didn't approve of this. "I like to give things an even break," he said, "Landing next to a bear with an airplane isn't fair chase," he said.

Before World War II, with dog teams he made several polar bear hunts on the ice of the Beaufort Sea, near Barter Island, off the northern coast of Alaska. He wasn't enthused over it. "It's cold and miserable," he said. "You never know when the ice is going to shift, and you could wind up in a strange country without a passport.

"On one hunt, a client wanted to shoot a polar bear, so I hired a young Eskimo with his dog team and the three of us traveled across the sea ice to hunt for a bear about nine miles off shore. The client wanted to go farther out," he told me. "However, the Eskimo warned, 'I don't think that's a good idea. My Daddy got caught on the ice, and he hasn't come back yet.'"

Slim asked, "How long has that been?"

"Three years," answered the Eskimo.

Slim looked at his hunter and said, "I don't want to join his father on one of those three year deals. Let's go this way."

He often said, "The killing isn't the whole thing on a hunt." He had in mind the enjoyment that comes from being in wilderness, the challenge to find top quality trophies, the thrill of living among wildlife, and the fellowship in camp and on the trail.

This is Slim Moore's book. I've had the honor of putting it together. I think the fifty plus years that have passed since I recorded it make it a more interesting story. I like to think of it as a fragment of the history of guided hunting in Alaska in the early 20th century.

—JIM REARDEN
Sprucewood
Homer, Alaska

When Hollywood Came to Alaska

"I WANT YOU TO GET US SOME LIVE WOLVERINES," movie director, Norman Don, said. He wore knickers. A golf cap drooped over one ear. A long cigarette holder, sometimes with a cigarette in it, grew from his chubby face.

"Wolverines?" I repeated foolishly, stalling for time. I scratched my head like I wasn't sure what a wolverine was.

"Yes. Half a dozen or so will do I guess," the little fellow allowed. "Tell your trapper friends we'll pay $250 for the first one, and $200 each for the others." It was late fall, 1935. Wolverine skins were worth $15 to $20, and a dollar was worth 100 valuable pennies.

Those were my first orders on the wackiest job I've ever had. I had just signed as animal man for Universal Pictures, a Hollywood movie outfit that had come to Alaska to shoot, as they say, on location. Norman Don had brought two assistants and an actor with him, as well as three stateside black bear cubs.

At the time, I guided non-resident hunters on big game hunts, ran a trapline winters, and during summers wrangled horses to pack supplies to mines in the Alaska Range. I had just returned from guiding a hunt for Fred Hollander, a nationally known sportsman and naturalist, when I ran into Norman Don at Fairbanks. He offered me twenty bucks a day plus expenses. It was good money then.

I thought I was qualified for the animal man job. If I had known a little about lion taming, and was a trapeze artist to boot, I've have been more qualified.

The fine movie Eskimo, written by Peter Freuchen, an expert on the Arctic, had appeared a couple of years earlier. I met Freuchen while he was in Alaska helping with that film, and I even took him fishing. He was a rugged man with a magnificent personality.

Tundra was the first name they hung on the film I was involved with; later they called it Arctic Fury. It was a low budget job, and was made on the peculiar theory that success of the magnificent Eskimo insured success of any far-north movie that followed.

"We're making a gen-u-wine Alaska movie. There'll be nothing phony about it," he swore, looking me in the eye.

I had just agreed to take the job and had shaken hands with him on it when he ordered the wolverines.

The story, or plot, was about a doctor, or as I used to call him, the bad actor, was supposed to have been forced down on the northern ice cap while flying his small plane across Alaska. He was walking across Alaska to civilization. A plague had killed all the Natives in the villages he came to, and he got into trouble everywhere he went. To top it off, a huge tundra fire chased him almost to the state of Washington. At first we filmed in Graehl, on the outskirts of Fairbanks, where carpenters built some false building fronts that supposedly represented Native villages. When the bad actor—the doctor that is—arrived at this village, it was supposedly filled with wild, starving dogs. We got a bunch of pooches, mostly sled dogs, from Jeff Studdard and Mike Agbaba, and other local mushers. With the sound track off, we'd call the dogs, and these nice fat dogs with wagging tails would show up around the false fronts for the cameraman to film. Any viewer could tell they weren't wild or starving, but Norman Don didn't seem to care.

Don wanted to film some caribou, so he hired about every bus in Fairbanks and filled them with anyone he could hire for the day. They were mostly winos and street people without jobs, and we went out to Nome Creek near the Steese Highway. The hired-for-the-day workers were supposed to herd caribou past the 300-pound stationary camera. The caribou had ideas of their own.

The starving doctor was supposed to chase caribou with a club as they fled past the camera. Where the director got the idea that a starving man with a club could catch and kill a caribou was beyond me, but it was typical of the thinking behind that film.

Using a 35mm Eyemo camera, I got a few caribou pictures. Norman Don decided to use a blue screen with my film and have the guy chase caribou with the club after they got back to Hollywood.

"A gen-u-wine Alaska movie," the director had said. I had to laugh when I learned of the crazy plot. It was typical Hollywood nonsense.

While we were in Fairbanks, I applied for and received a permit from game warden Sam O. White to capture and hold wild animals. I asked Norman Don what justification to use for the permit. "Educational purposes," he said. With a straight face he explained, "The film will educate people in the States about Alaska."

I have since often wondered if Norman Don's film is where folks in the South-48 got some of their bizarre ideas about Alaska.

As fall waned, Fairbanks temperatures started to drop. In hopes of milder temperatures, the production was moved to Anchorage, then a tiny railroad and fishing village surrounded by good moose, sheep, and bear country. Today Anchorage and vicinity has several hundred thousand residents milling in and around paved streets and modern buildings.

We hired carpenters to build cages and pens for all the animals we planned to collect. While they were working, I decided to try to pick up a couple of wolverine. In the meantime, I spread the word to back-country trappers that we wanted live wolverines.

I took a small outfit and back-packed up the old Crow Creek Trail on the Kenai Peninsula, near Girdwood. It's an old dog team and horse mail route, historically used by packers and foot travelers.

Snow had covered the high ridges and mountains where, on snowshoes, I prowled for several days, hunting wolverine sign.

I found where one had passed, followed his wallowing trail in new snow for a few miles, and found a suitable place to make several blind sets with padded number four Newhouse double-spring traps.

Next day, I lugged to the same area a fresh moose head someone had left near the old trail. This I wired to a tree a couple of feet off the ground, and set a couple of my padded traps beneath it in the snow, with waxed paper over the trap pans.

I expected the wolverine to find the head and start tugging on it. It wouldn't move, and the more he pulled, the angrier he would become, until he'd forget and step into a trap.

Four days later I snowshoed to the moose head and found an angry, beady-eyed wolverine there, caught by a front foot. The bandy-legged little devil growled and crouched to leap at me when I got near.

I backed off.

A wolverine is an unfriendly cuss at best; when you're trying to pack him out of the hills and stuff him into a pen alive he's damn near impossible. I didn't dare tap him on the nose to knock him cold—I might have hit him too hard.

"You won't buffalo me, you little so-and-so," I told him.

I fastened another padded trap to a pole and fished until I caught one of his rear paws, then I stretched him as tightly as I could. I figured I had him then. I went to tape his jaws shut, but every time I got near, he yanked and struggled and growled and turned his head and those big popping ivories my way. A wolverine can bite through bone, a pole, and even wire. I sure didn't want him chomping on me.

If you don't think a wolverine is quick, just try to pick a live one out of a trap yourself. I guarantee your hackles will crawl. His growls sound very sincere.

I finally mushed to my camp for a big tarp, which I doubled until I had about six thicknesses. I threw it over him, then lay on it. He couldn't bite through the canvas. But he roared, turned, and twisted frantically under me.

I groped through one layer of canvas at a time, found his head through the canvas and pinned it down. I peeled the edge of the tarp back so I could grab his snoot. An animal doesn't have much strength in opening its jaws; when they close them it's another matter. I carefully grabbed his jaws with one hand, held them closed, and wrapped adhesive tape around them with the other.

He hummed and growled and snuffled noisily through his

nose, calling me an ugly, no-good two-legged stinker. I grinned and stood up. He batted his nose against my leg, trying to bite.

I slid my packboard under him, wrapped each ivory-clawed foot in adhesive tape, and with stout cord lashed his feet to the corners.

I slipped into the shoulder straps, got into my webs, and headed for camp. He weighed about twenty-five pounds. He pumped himself up and down with all his strength. That animal was twenty-five pounds of powerful coiled spring.

I weaved down the trail like a drunk. Because of his violent pumping, it was all I could do to stand. As he pumped he skidded his cold nose up and down the back of my neck, growling, mumbling, and snuffling. The hair on the back of my neck came up like teeth on a comb, and shivers chased each other up and down my spine.

I BEGAN TO WONDER how thoroughly I had taped his jaws, and stopped and wrapped another half spool of tape on them. It made me feel more secure, but the chills still prickled my spine when he ran that wet nose along my neck, and growled and rumbled into my ears.

I packed him to Girdwood and put him in a barrel. I cut one foot loose at a time until he was free. At the last instant I slipped my knife under the tape on one side of his head. He could then claw the tape off. I then clapped a tin tub atop the barrel. A few days later I caught another. I hog-tied that one and shoved him into a sack, which I lashed to the packboard so he couldn't pump and couldn't get his nose on my neck.

I took my pets to Anchorage. The notices offering big money for wolverines had started to bring results. Soon we had eight live, growling, and cussing wolverines in our pens.

A couple died within twenty-four hours; I skinned one of these and found a bashed-in skull. I grinned when I saw that, thinking of the time I had getting my first one out of a trap alive and uninjured.

A big guy brought one from Seward. He was a regular wild-west-appearing character, with firearms and knives strapped on him until you'd think he was going to a Mexican revolution. His black whiskers reached clear to his belt. And he had two big buckets of porcupine meat.

"Wolverines won't eat nothin' but porky meat," he declared.

But what I remember most clearly, and what I've puzzled over for years, is the cage that held his wolverine. It was a beautifully-built miniature log cabin, barely big enough to hold the wolverine. It had no door. We had to tear the cage apart to let it out.

How did he get the wolverine into that thing? I wish I had asked.

We first kept the wolverines in cages designed for the three black bear cubs Norman Don had brought with him. They were stout, and lined with metal. But after we had more wolverines than we had bear cages, the director, against my advice, decided wolverines weren't such fierce critters after all, so he had plywood cages built for them, with three thicknesses of mink wire (used on mink farm pens) for doors.

These kept the wolverines fine for three or four days. But one morning as I started to open the door to the garage where we had the wolverine cages, what sounded like a pack of loose wolverines slammed against the door crack, fighting each other and the door to get out. They had chewed through the wire doors.

I nearly jerked the door off its hinges getting it closed. I didn't know how many animals were loose. From the noises they made it could have been all six.

The cold sweat popped out on me, and I half considered resigning and heading for the hills and my trapline, where the only wolverines I had to deal with were those I could bam across the nose with a club.

That was when I could have used a little lion-taming experience.

I had a snare-pole for handling the bear cubs. One, which weighed about 100 pounds, was pretty ornery. We called her Madame Queen, and we had to be careful around her. Her teeth and claws were always ready.

All three of the cubs were about half tame, and just as sure as we turned them loose to do some filming, they got cold feet in the snow, and scrambled up a tree. It was my job, of course, to get 'em down.

A little skill as a trapeze artist might have helped on that little job.

It was impossible to climb past the bears. When I tried it, they slapped and bit me like wildcats. Since I was hanging on to the tree with everything I had, I couldn't turn loose to bat back at them. So, instead of climbing above them and pushing them down, I rigged a shovel handle with a snare of airplane cable. With that I could keep my distance and snatch them back to earth.

I tried to do it gently.

I decided to recapture the loose wolverines with the snare-pole. But first, I scouted for someone to help. The first guy I found was the cameraman.

"Say, uh, I wonder if you could help me for a few minutes?" I asked.

"Sure, Slim. What's up?" he asked.

"Well, uh, some of the wolverines are loose in the garage, and . . ."

He was silent for a long time, staring at me. Finally, he said, nervous like, "Gosh, Slim, I don't know anything about wolverines. Maybe you'd better get someone else."

It took all my powers of persuasion to get him to help.

We found several empty oil drums and worked them through the door and into the garage, and stood behind them for protection. The instant we cracked the door three wolverines hit the barrels, but we were ready and braced. The noise they made was enough to curl your hair. The cameraman was pale, and I thought he was going to scram, but he had guts and stayed.

When we yelled, the wolverines retreated. They growled and cussed, and in general raised hell. I was relieved to find only three were loose.

Once inside, we closed the door behind us and stood behind the barrels. One of them dashed toward us and came close enough for me to slip the loop over his head. I held the snare pretty tight. That hot-tempered little cuss got pretty tame before I dropped him into one of the barrels and covered it.

One of the remaining two charged and bounced off the barrels repeatedly, and dashed around so fast I couldn't get the snare on him. The third wolverine spent most of the time crouched under a bench growling.

Finally, the crazy one dashed by. On impulse, I dropped the snare and grabbed both his hind feet and picked him up. He started to double over and reach for me, and I automatically spun to keep him away.

By the time I had whirled him around a couple of times, I wished I hadn't been so impulsive. It wasn't exactly like having a tiger by the tail, but it was pretty close. I couldn't stop spinning long enough to drop him into a barrel.

As the wolverine and I went around and around I saw the cameraman's face peeking over a barrel. His eyes were like saucers. He ducked every time the wolverine swished past, and I guess he was afraid I'd turn loose and dump the roaring critter on him.

After half a dozen spins I became dizzy. I was beginning to wonder how it would end when I staggered a bit, trying to keep my feet. As I staggered I moved closer to a post in the garage and the next time around the wolverine's head slammed against it. That took most of the fight out of him, and it was easy to drop him into a barrel. I hadn't intended such rugged treatment, but it did take that the tiger out of my hands, so to speak.

I tottered dizzily to the barrels and waited until the garage quit spinning before going after the third animal. He was still under the bench. I got the snare around his neck and pulled him into the open. He braced his feet, growling, but I skidded him out anyway.

I hated to lift him by the neck with the snare, so I asked the cameraman to lift his body while I kept the snare tight and controlled his head.

The cameraman later accused me of turning the wolverine loose on purpose, but I didn't. So help me, it was accidental.

He grabbed the growling critter's tail and pulled, stretching the body tight. He intended to put one hand underneath and support most of the weight by the belly, while I lifted the head with the snare; we would drop it into a barrel together.

As he pulled on the tail, somehow the quick little devil pulled out of the noose. I don't know how he did it. One moment I had him, the next he was out. This put the cameraman in an awkward position. He had a wolverine by the tail.

I guess he remembered how I had handled the situation earlier. Anyway, he started to whirl. At the same time he yelled, adding his excited voice to the growls of the angry wolverine.

With each spin the cameraman took a couple of steps toward the post where I had clonked my wolverine. His intent was obvious.

Now, I was responsible for those animals. I took my work seriously. I didn't want all my wolverines to wind up with bashed-in heads. I hadn't slammed mine against the pole purposely, though I suspect the cameraman thought I had.

I decided the only way out was to have the cameraman release the animal, so I yelled, "Turn him loose."

He took me at my word, but his timing was bad—or good, depending how you look at it. He claimed later it was to retaliate for my having slacked off on the noose. Anyway, the wolverine catapulted directly toward me. I flung myself down and I swear it brushed me as it flew by. I heard it bounce off the garage wall and ricochet off one of the three barrels we had by the door.

I got to my feet and turned to see it staggering toward me. I don't believe that wolverine knew where it was going, but it was sure trying to go. Automatically I held the snare-pole out, and he rammed his head into the noose as if on purpose. I jerked it tight, and without any more humane ideas of having the cameraman lift him with me, heaved upward as if he were a big fish and dropped him into the last empty barrel. We slammed the lid on it.

In a moment we were laughing. We may even have been a bit hysterical. It was funny only in retrospect.

The only actor in the film, Del Cameron, played the role of the doctor. He was a 200-pound bruiser who didn't like any part of being in Alaska. We had quite a time with him when it came to the wolverines. Getting him to go into a pen and act with them running around growling and fighting each other, and threatening him, was almost impossible; I guess he figured they were bad actors.

Every time one ran toward him with the apparent intent of

sampling some raw Hollywood meat, he cringed and backed up. He also raised the club he insisted on carrying. He was thoroughly and genuinely scared, and I didn't blame him.

"Magnificent acting; did you get that?" the director yelled at the cameraman while the poor guy danced around defending himself. Acting was the last thing he had in mind at such times.

I once had the temerity to approach the director to point out, since we were filming a "gen-u-wine Alaska movie," that wolverines don't run around in packs. The shrug and explanation that we needed more action didn't satisfy me, but I let it go.

The wolverines got meaner and harder for me to catch every time we turned them into the pen for filming. I was almost as happy as the actor when the wolverine sequences ended and I could take them out of town to turn them loose.

A number of young and pretty Anchorage girls often came to watch the filming. The director allowed one or the other to hold up a board with the number of the scene on it, while the photographer exposed film on it. After that, the girls arrived dressed fit to kill, thinking maybe there would be a scout there to take them to Hollywood. Didn't happen.

The director wanted it to appear that there were many animals being chased by the fire. The fleeing doctor somehow adopted two black bear cubs who supposedly traveled with him as he fled a huge wildfire. The actor was in a pen which appeared to be in the woods. We had a huge fire burning nearby. He was supposed to grab a cub and rush off, saving the poor orphaned animal from the fire.

We had dropped a tree on the cub a few hours earlier. The poor little bears didn't know what to expect; one minute we petted them and fed them goodies, the next we exposed them to smoke and fire, dropped trees on them, and manhandled them kind of roughly.

When the actor ran to grab the cub it happened to be Madam Queen, the mean one. She came up on her hind feet, snorted, peeled her lips, and chomped away on the actor's arm. At the same time, she clawed the poor man. She must have pinched a dozen blood blisters on his arm, and he had scratches all over his back. His clothing, torn to fit the story line, was even more torn where the cub had ripped it.

He dropped the cub. The director yelled, "Pick him up and carry him off."

The actor refused. "To hell with it," he fumed.

The director than jumped and down and screamed, "Do it!" and angrily threw his long cigarette holder into the snow.

His act topped that of the actor, and the actor reluctantly managed to pick the cub up and carry her off camera.

It then took an assistant an hour or two of digging through snow to find the cigarette holder.

The director rented 200 mink from a mink rancher near Anchorage. They were released in an auditorium that was camouflaged to look like woodlands.

We strung lights around the bottom of the auditorium for the filming. The cameraman decided to use overhead lights instead. Someone came up with the bright idea of removing the bottom bulbs. Unfortunately, the juice was left on. In the midst of filming, half a dozen mink stuck their noses into the empty light sockets and were electrocuted. I skinned them and presented the skins to the director.

The director wanted even more animals in the scenes. At the time, the easiest animals to acquire in large numbers were porcupines. The nearby Kenai Peninsula was loaded with them; fox and mink ranchers fed them to their animals by the hundreds.

When the director offered five dollars each for live porcupines, plus cost of freight to Anchorage, they arrived in a veritable flood; we had 300 of them before we could stop the onslaught. They were in boxes, pens, barrels, cages, woodsheds, car trunks, and anything else we could stuff them into.

To simulate the huge tundra fire, a gang was hired to cut dry spruce trees, which we piled high, saturated with diesel oil, and set afire. We turned the porkies loose and the camera started rolling.

Instead of fleeing the fire, as often as not they ran into it. Regardless of what we did, they refused to perform for the camera.

Someone (not me) came up with the idea of making tin chutes to slide the porkies down. Then, so the plan went, they would scuttle past the stationary camera. Billowing smoke hid the chutes from the camera.

The smoke nearly asphyxiated us. Our eyes watered so badly we couldn't see much. And have you ever tried to shove a live porcupine, head first, down a slick metal chute where it doesn't want to go?

We got the porkies to the bottom of the chutes by using snare poles, heavy gloves (which the quills often penetrated), and plenty of cussing. They dropped to the ground and some stood stupidly to have the next porky drop on top of them; the one on top got a bunch of quills in its belly.

Porky feed was a problem. We spent a lot of time cutting boughs and brush from which they ate the bark. Our outfit stayed at an old homestead ranch belonging to H. P. Allen. Naturally, we called him "High Power." And old High Power had about three tons of rutabagas left from the previous summer's garden crop. His sales pitch convinced the director they were just the thing to feed the porkies. He sold him the entire lot.

As it happened, they liked and ate 'em fine. The trouble was, they were "high power" too; the resulting diarrhea killed many porkies.

In desperation, we hung dead and frozen porkies from piano wire and put a guy back in the brush to pull the wire and yank them across in front of the camera. They bumped and bounced across the snow and ice, their feet swinging back and forth. When the film was developed, they looked more natural than the live ones; they really seemed to trot across the screen.

At one time a couple of the bear cubs were in the same pen as a bunch of porkies. Both ran up to a porky or two, and the both got quills in their noses.

It took four of us to pull those quills. One man held the hind feet, another the front feet, and a third the head, while the fourth guy, with pliers, yanked quills. I held the front feet on one, and he kept easing his feet to his mouth, trying to chew my thumbs. I could hold him all right, but I almost had to hurt the poor cub to do so. Those little guys were strong.

Then there were the birds. He decided the little fish crows from Latouche Island, in Prince William Sound, were exactly what he wanted. He bought several hundred that obliging Natives trapped.

The fact that crows don't exist in the area the "doctor" was supposedly in made no difference.

We photographed the crows while they were in covered fox pens. Smoke blew past, upsetting the little black squawkers, and they hollered and fluttered and acted fine.

When we were through with them, the soft-hearted director ordered me to turn them loose. Crows are not native to Anchorage.

At the same time we were finished with the porcupines, so he ordered me to release them too.

It was bedlam. For a few days there was a porcupine or three in every tree in town. About every other dog in town had a sore face where quills had been pulled.

One old-timer, with blood in his eye, looked us up with a shotgun under his arm. He had been awakened before daylight that morning by a rattling and crunching on his front porch. He rolled out of a warm bed, poked a flashlight and shotgun out the front door, and found a porcupine busily gnawing on a post on his porch.

The director bought him off with a fistful of cash.

The little rowdy loud-mouth fish crows darted around Anchorage for quite a while. They were confused, and went in gangs. Some of the local shotgun artists had some great wing shooting for a while. This burned up the more staid citizens.

They blamed us, of course.

One of the more ardent wing shots knocked down a high-flying crow during one of our filming sessions. From a cloud of black feathers, the dead crow tumbled through the air and landed with a loud "whump" twenty feet from the actor, who was busily hamming up a scene. His startled look toward the dead crow made the director yell, "Cut."

I was admiring the guy's great shot when the director yelled, "Slim, will you go see what you can do about the wise guy with the shotgun?"

He had faded by the time I got to the spot from which he had shot. It did give me a chance to get away where I could laugh.

I accidentally caught a couple of falcons in some padded traps I had set for rabbits (snowshoe hare). I've always figured a falcon had a lot of nerve, but I saw an interesting demonstration that indicated otherwise.

Someone had sent us a bald eagle. It had injured a wing, and could fly but a short distance. One day, with the two falcons in a fox pen, there was to be some sort of a scene with the eagle, which wasn't very wild. I picked him off his perch, pulled his wings over his back and released him in the pen with the falcons, which were sitting on perches.

As the eagle flew around inside the little pen, the two falcons screamed bloody murder, and, so help me, one of them fainted. It fell off its perch, and lay limply on the ground. I suppose that when falcons are free, they figure they're ok; but close up and being confined with the eagle was too much for one of them.

The eagle became a scene stealer one day. He was on a perch inside the acting pen while the actor was trying to catch a rabbit. Maybe the actor's clumsy attempts disgusted him. Anyway, as the actor bent over reaching for a rabbit he had cornered, he flew to the actor and landed on his back.

The actor froze in a stooped over position. "Get him off there," he yelled.

I knew if I picked the eagle up, the bird would tighten his claws, giving the actor an honest something to yell about.

"Lie down and roll over," I yelled.

The actor responded to my order a lot faster than he had for a lot of instructions he had received from the director. When he flopped on the ground, the eagle calmly stepped off.

Meanwhile, of course, the rabbit had skedaddled to the other side of the pen.

When the actor finally managed to club a rabbit and pick its limp body up, the scene was broken, and he was given some fried chicken to eat in front of the camera. He really hammed it up in that scene.

I'd have turned down the job as animal man if I had known what was involved. As it was, I tried to give the best care I could to the captive animals, with plenty of food and water. The cages and pens weren't the best, but they mostly kept the animals secure.

Norman Don was soft-hearted, and gave me a lot of leeway.

As soon as the filming for each of the animals was completed, he let me take them out of town to release them, or in some cases, I released them right in town. I got more pleasure out of that than I did in handling them as captives.

That was a hilarious four months. Sometimes I laughed, and then again I was ashamed to be mixed up with a thing like that. Finally, as they say in Hollywood, the film was in the can.

I've been asked what I thought of the finished film. To be honest, I've never seen it.

[AUTHOR: An abbreviated form of this story appeared in *The Alaska Sportsman* magazine in March, 1966; it also appeared in that form in my book *Jim Rearden's Alaska, Fifty Years of Frontier Adventure*. The version in this volume is full length—the way Slim told it to me in December, 1956.]

M. W. (Slim) Moore

AUTHOR: MORRIS WILSON (SLIM) MOORE (few of his friends knew his name was Morris; he was always "Slim," even in the phone directory) was born April 8, 1898, in Eastland County, Texas. He grew up in Texas and the Southwest. He once told me he was "... raised by Ma Bell" (Southern Bell Telephone), and that he spent his 16th, 17th, and 18th, birthdays working on a line truck.

He sailed steerage class from Seattle to Cordova, Alaska, in March, 1926 and worked as a lineman on the tram run between Bonanza Mine and the Kennecott copper mill. In May, 1927, he walked the 275 miles from Chitina to Fairbanks and went to work for the gold-mining Fairbanks Exploration Company as a lineman and electrician.

During winters he hunted and trapped. In the summer of 1929 he and five other prospectors mined gold in Miller's Gulch, near the headwaters of the Alaska Range's Chistochina River.

"We came out that fall to find everyone talking about the depression," Slim told me. "We didn't know what they were talking about. We'd lived in a depression all summer."

He left his job as an electrician in 1927, and moved into the high Alaska Range near Miller, eighteen miles north of Summit Lake, to trap, build cabins, and cut trails. He also became a commercial back-packer, carrying supplies on his back into mining camps at the headwaters of the Alaska Range Gakona River. Sup-

Nine brown bears, fishing at McNeil River falls. These bears have become accustomed to seeing human viewers, provided the human keep to their regular areas. In the early 1950s Slim Moore urged the Alaska Game Commission to close this area to hunting, and to set it aside for viewing. JAMES FARO

plies were freighted over the Valdez Trail (Richardson Highway) and Slim picked them up in the vicinity of Paxson and Summit Lakes. He then back-packed them to mines twenty-five to forty miles distant, across the divide that lies between the Gulkana and Gakona Rivers.

He once contracted to pack supplies to the Slate Creek mine of Ed Stroecker, founder of the First National Bank of Fairbanks. Much of one shipment consisted of 100-pound kegs filled with bolts, spikes, and hardware. Slim made a shoulder yoke, and carried a keg on each side (200 pounds in all) across the mountains and tundra to Stroecker's mine.

In 1931 he became a licensed big game hunting guide. He was one of the few guides who were licensed to guide anywhere in the Territory. Most were limited to specific regions. It is difficult today to convey the respect Alaskans had for the Territory's fifty or so registered guides of the 1930s. Each was an unpaid deputized game warden, silver badge and all. Guide examinations were difficult, and only part of the requirements. Alaska Game Commission wardens (officially wildlife agents after 1939) who issued guide licenses always personally knew the candidates and their reputations. Only ethical and competent men of good reputation became licensed guides.

Slim acquired a string of packhorses in 1932, after which he spent summers letting the horses pack the supplies to various mines, and to geological survey crews. During fall hunting season he used the horses to take client hunters afield in the Alaska Range to hunt moose, caribou, bear, and Dall sheep trophies.

In 1940, Slim filed for a business site at Summit Lake, an above-timberline (elevation 3,210 feet) clear-water jewel of a lake on the Richardson Highway. He received final patent for the land in 1950. He first built a cabin, and later his Summit Lake Lodge there. The lodge was a small neat establishment offering cabins, gasoline, and a restaurant. It was the only lodge above timberline on the Richardson Highway, and continued in business for many years after Slim sold it in 1962. It finally burned to the ground, and has never been rebuilt.

In 1938, his income from guiding and trapping was down, for the depression had impacted his usual businessman clients, and Slim moved to Fairbanks. Through World War II years he worked as a Pole Line Foreman at the military Ladd Field, at Fairbanks. He set many poles and constructed many miles of electric distribution and secondary power lines. In 1947, while climbing a power pole, the pole snapped at the ground and fell with Slim, breaking his back, and ending his pole climbing days.

On recovering, Slim built his Summit Lake Lodge. The guiding business in Alaska picked up in the 1950s, and boomed in the 1960s and 1970s, when many guides booked dozens of clients and farmed them out to assistant guides on their payrolls. For some, it became a free-wheeling million-dollar business, with huge lodges, airplanes, and camps scattered far across Alaska.

19 M. W. (SLIM) MOORE

A fine big brown bear eating a salmon it caught at McNeil falls. Most photos and movies of brown bears seen in publications and films over the past four decades were taken at McNeil River. JAMES FARO

That wasn't Slim's way. His hunts were personalized, old-fashioned, tent-camping outings. When he contracted to take a hunter after game, he was there to see the hunter received a superior hunt, and good care. His hunters appreciated it. One, W.E.Young, Sr, a Texan, described his adventures on a thirty-day hunt with Slim in "Hunt of a Lifetime," that appeared in the November, 1949 Alaska Sportsman magazine. Of Slim, Young said, ". . . he's the best guide and one of the finest fellows I've ever met."

Warren Tilman, another top guide of Slim's era, who at times partnered in guiding with Slim, once told me, "Slim is like a hungry Indian when he gets on the trail of a good trophy. He stays with it until his hunter gets it or quits."

Slim's ethics were of the highest, whether it be while hunting, or something else. In the early 1960's, as a registered guide, I guided Mr. and Mrs. Philip Neuweiler, of Allentown, Pennsylvania, owners of a brewery, on a month-long hunt for sheep, caribou, brown bear, and moose. They were ideal clients who enjoyed the wilderness, and took quality trophies.

The Neuweiler's wanted to return to hunt with me the following year, but I had accepted a position as a biologist with the Alaska Department of Fish and Game, and I could no longer guide because of a conflict of interest.

As a favor, I asked Slim to book the Neuweilers for a hunt. He did, and they became his main clients for the remainder of his guiding years.

I didn't see Slim for a couple of years. When I did he said, "Jim, I owe you some money. I've set it aside in the bank, but haven't gotten around to sending it to you."

I was amazed. "For what, Slim?"

"Ten percent of the fees I've been collecting from the Neuweilers," he explained.

We had no such understanding. I laughed at him. "You did me a favor. I wanted the Neuweilers to have the best guide in the state, and they got him. You owe me nothing."

Slim knew I would refuse the money. He was so ethical he offered it anyway.

Phil Neuweiler made at least thirty month-long fall big game

Slim, in December, 1956, at home in the log cabin he built at Summit Lake. He hauled the logs with a dog team from the Paxon area.
JIM REARDEN

hunts in Canada and Alaska before he hunted with me. He was in his fifties and sixties when he hunted with Slim. In his book, *Big Game Trails in the Far North* (Great Northwest Publishing and Distributing Company, Inc., Anchorage, 1989) Neuweiler wrote admiringly of Slim, "Slim and I could be left in any territory, under any conditions, and find and take as much game as any two young guys. We know where to look for game. If there is any game in the area we can find it, and, with a spotting scope, we can tell if it is good, and if it's no good we don't go after it."

Neuweiler wrote that it sometimes took some time for he and Slim to catch up with a trophy: "In the Aleutians, we found the tracks of a tremendous brown bear. We knew he was a great big bear, and I knew I wanted him. We hunted him three years before we caught up with him, and we turned down a lot of other bears while we were doing it. But we eventually got him because we had the patience."

He called Slim, "... an outfitter, the best in the whole world, and one of the top ten story-tellers in the North Country."

In the early 1950s Slim took a client to McNeil River, a large stream that pours into the west side of lower Cook Inlet. There he found an almost unheard of concentration of brown bears fishing for salmon.

"Bears were everywhere. There was almost no hunting to it; I picked out the biggest and my hunter shot it," he told me.

He recommended that the Alaska Game Commission (the Territory's wildlife rule-making body) close the area to brown bear hunting. "It's the perfect place for bear viewing," he argued.

When Slim spoke, people listened. It probably helped that famed guide Andy Simon, a member of the Game Commission for twenty-eight years, was, for a time, Slim's father-in-law and a good friend. In 1955 the Game Commission accepted Slim's recommendation and closed the McNeil River area to bear hunting, a giant step in pre-statehood days. The closure has continued to this day, and McNeil River is now world-famous for viewing bears, thanks to the forethought of Slim Moore.

Many of the quality photos of brown bears seen on TV and in magazines and books are taken there, where as many as fifty or sixty brownies may be seen fishing for salmon at the same time.

In the 1970s a handful of guides hunting the Alaska Peninsula illegally flew small planes to spot brown bears from the air, and landed their clients near the bears to shoot them. Some left their clients on the ground with a rifle, and, with their airplanes, drove the bears to the "hunters."

During a Board of Fish and Game public hearing, many ethical guides as well as sportsmen, complained about this. Slim's testimony was the most memorable. He referred disparagingly to these pilot-guides as "crop dusters." After that, it was the term Board members used while discussing the issue.

I was a member of the Board of Fish and Game at the time, and proposed a regulation that would prohibit hunters throughout Alaska from taking big game on the same day they are airborne. At first, the Board rejected it; they also rejected it upon my second try a year later. But they adopted it as a regulation (law) the third time I made the proposal. Today, going on four decades later, it is still an enforced regulation throughout Alaska. To stay legal, you don't shoot any big game animal on the same day you've been airborne.

Slim's "crop duster" comment played an important part in my repeatedly reminding the Board of the misuse of airplanes in hunting, and in the eventual adoption of the no-hunting-on-the-same-day- airborne regulation.

Professional wildlife biologists often consulted with Slim about wildlife problems and regulatory solutions. His knowledge of Alaska's fauna was encyclopedic, and over the years many of his suggestions for regulations were adopted by the Territory, and later, the State.

Slim, about 1972, when he lived in Anchorage. JIM REARDEN

Slim Moore had hundreds of admiring friends. He was named Alaska's Guide of the Year in 1973 by the Alaska Professional Hunters Association (professional hunting guides). In 1974 APHA presented him with the Simon-Waugh award, its highest honor; only three other guides had received it. In 1978 the Alaska Legislature awarded him an honorary Master Guide License for Life, and congratulated him in a formal resolution for his almost half a century of guiding. When he retired at 80, he was the oldest active guide in Alaska.

He died in Anchorage in April, 1982, at 83.

His trail was straight.

3
Riding a Ram Down a Mountain

I HADN'T BEEN IN ALASKA VERY LONG, when one December, during late sheep season, Elmer Nelson and I decided to kill a couple of Dall rams, thinking they'd be good to eat. Elmer and I came into Alaska together, and in the early years we often trapped and hunted together. We were wrong about sheep meat in December. The rams we killed were skinny, and the meat was poor. We took them at the wrong time. When killed earlier in the year there isn't a finer meat than that of a Dall ram.

We lived near Paxson's, in the Alaska Range, and there were sheep mountains all around us. We took my dog team and searched until we spotted two rams not too far up a mountainside, then eased up the fairly steep slope, through a little snow, keeping among big rocks for cover. The two rams we had spotted were digging through snow and feeding near the head of a high draw. We were within about 200 yards when both of us shot, and both rams fell.

We decided the easy way to get them off the mountain was to take them down the bottom of the draw, which was filled with hard-packed snow, topped by a few inches of fresh snow.

We had tied my dog team about half way up the ridge. After shooting, we returned for the dogs, thinking we'd use them to skid the rams down the draw. Leaving the sled where it was, and harnesses on the dogs, with the dogs loose and following, we worked our way up the draw until it became too steep for easy climbing.

Slim, in the 1930s, with a nice Dall ram. "A Dall sheep isn't awfully bright, but it lives in a country where the going is pretty rough for other animals," said Slim. ROSEMARIE OLSEN

The dogs and I waited while Elmer worked the rest of the way to the dead rams. "I'll kick 'em loose," he said. "I might even ride one of 'em down," he grinned.

I thought he was kidding.

He cut steps in the steep, hard-drifted snow, and slowly climbed out of sight. I waited for quite a while, knowing he was taking time to gut the rams.

Finally, I heard a little rumble, and here, above me, came one of the rams, skidding around a bend. It must have been doing thirty miles an hour. It ran up the side of that turn like a man on a motorcycle in a motor-drome, and whizzed down the far side of the draw.

Soon, here came the other ram, the same way, sliding high on the turn, and plunging past me. Both rams still had their horns when they went by, but that didn't seem to be slowing them down.

After the rams went by, Elmer was gone so long I began to worry, but he finally worked his way down to me, one careful step at a time. With the dogs, we climbed down to where the rams had stopped. It was still a long way to the bottom, and plenty steep, too. However, it was a straight shot filled with hard-packed snow. It seemed to be clear of boulders.

"Let's ride 'em to the bottom from here," Elmer suggested. It was kind of a dare, but it looked possible.

"I'll be right behind you," I agreed, after thinking it over. Neither of us wanted to pack meat out of that steep draw. Footing was poor, and the sides were steep.

He straddled a ram, grabbed the horns, pulled them back so they wouldn't drag, and shoved off. He plunged down that steep slope as if he were riding a bobsled; he really traveled.

It looked like fun, but it looked dangerous too.

I climbed aboard the other ram, grabbed the horns, and followed him.

Elmer was probably fifty yards ahead of me when I saw him bounce over a little hump. When I got to the spot, I saw and grabbed a sheep's foot that stuck out of the snow. It almost jerked me off of my mount. It was a lamb that had been caught by a snow slide, and Elmer had knocked it loose as he skidded across it.

We traveled so fast the dogs couldn't begin to keep up. As I clung to that ram's horns and zipped downhill, snow beneath and around me became a blur, and the wind in my face was so strong it made my eyes water. Fresh snow atop packed snow creates a slippery surface, and we flew down that near-vertical draw as if we were on ball bearings. I'll bet our speed reached fifty miles an hour.

After we reached bottom and stopped, I tossed the lamb toward Elmer, explaining, "I picked up an extra on the way down."

We sat and relaxed on the warm white rams and gazed up at the steep gully, almost not believing what we had done. Then we laughed, almost hysterically, because it was funny, and because we were happy to have made it without breaking anything or killing ourselves.

It was the easiest time I ever had in getting dead rams out of the mountains, and the only time it was fun. It was scary fun, but fun nevertheless.

[AUTHOR'S NOTE: Slim told friends how he and Elmer rode the rams down the mountain, and the yarn became kind of a local legend. A few years later, an Alaska Game Commission warden of the time who later became a nationally-known outdoor writer, wrote a story for a national magazine describing how he and his hunting partner had ridden two just-killed rams down a mountain gully; Slim's name wasn't mentioned. Clearly, he had swiped Slims yarn, added fictional details, and sold it as a personal experience.]

Alaska's Dall sheep have always fascinated me, and I've long wanted to see what makes them tick. I used to pack supplies to gold mines and to Geological Survey crews in the Alaska Range. At first I packed the stuff on my back; later I had packhorses. I saw a lot of sheep while in this endeavor, for in those years their numbers in the Alaska Range were high. I often sat and watched them with the binoculars I always carried around my neck and tucked into my shirt.

I was fascinated by their ability to thrive on high, rugged mountains. However, sheep, like other animals, make mistakes. The lamb I picked up on my slide down the mountain is a good example. As good as they are at mountain survival, even they are occasionally caught in snow slides, or killed by predators.

At the time, one could get a permit from the Alaska Game Commission to kill sheep for food when prospecting, working at a remote mine, or even when packing. A sheep is small enough so all of it can usually be used before the meat spoils. In the spring, summer, and fall, active time for mining and surveying, much of the meat of a moose or caribou may spoil before an entire carcass can be utilized.

About eighty-five percent of Alaska's mountain sheep's food is arctic *Dryas*, a low, green, high mountain plant with crinkly leaves that never seems to grow higher than about four inches. I always open the stomachs of animals I kill to see what they've been eating. When you know what an animal feeds on, you know where to look for him. Rarely, I've found a bit of caribou moss (lichen) in a sheep; sometimes I've found bunch grass, or the leaves of dwarf willows, which the sheep come down into some of the higher draws to feed on. But the bulk of their food is *Dryas*, which grows best where sheep have bedded and left a lot of dung.

I suspect that may be why sheep meat is so fine eating. I've noticed that caribou I've killed high in the sheep hills often go for

Dryas in a big way. When I've found it in a caribou's stomach, it was about the best caribou meat I've ever eaten.

A Dall sheep isn't awfully bright, but he's in a country where the going is generally pretty rough for other animals. Though they live in the mountains, they feed mostly on gentle slopes where there is plenty of ground feed. Usually, there are rugged cliffs or canyon walls nearby where they can escape quickly from wolves or coyotes.

I hunted sheep in the Alaska Range regularly through the 1930s, and had a fair idea of their numbers. About the first part of World War II (the early 1940s) we kind of ran out of sheep. I think coyotes had a lot to do with it.

In spring, when ewes are lambing, there is generally too much snow for sheep in the higher mountains, and they have to move to lower elevations to find feed. On these lower benches, which aren't as rugged as the higher elevations, coyotes can more easily catch and kill lambs, as well as ewes.

Ewes lamb at about the same time as the coyotes have their pups. The coyotes need meat to support themselves and pups. This is good for coyotes, not so good for sheep.

Areas favorable for sheep are also favorable for coyotes. Both sheep and coyotes like wind-swept country. During winter, sheep favor hills where the wind blows the snow clear so they can find feed; they can't dig through deep snow like caribou do.

I hunted the same sheep areas for years, but I didn't hunt on the creeks where ewes and lambs live in the fall. Rams and ewes generally associate with each other only during the rut in late October and November. I hunted in ram country, and didn't pay much attention to the numbers of ewes and lambs. At the time, most of the coyote droppings I saw in the hills seemed to be filled with sheep hair, but I didn't think much about it until what seemed like all of a sudden we ran out of sheep. I think the old ones that escaped coyotes died off, and there weren't many to take their place.

The coyote was a newcomer to the Alaska Range in the 1930s. They were especially numerous in the late 1930s. In those years, in the sheep hills, I saw, and had chance to shoot at, quite a few of them. I hadn't noticed them in earlier years.

The rabbits (snowshoe hares) where I hunted in the Alaska

Range died off around 1937–38. After that, coyotes made it awfully hard for sheep to survive.

During World War II there was little sheep hunting, for no one had time. It was then that coyotes kind of disappeared; apparently something about interior Alaska isn't suitable for coyotes. They weren't trapped off; their numbers simply dwindled. A few remained around Delta and the Copper River country. They liked the Kenai Peninsula, and their numbers remain fairly high there. As they decreased in the Alaska Range, the sheep population started to recover.

About 1940 I was having dinner with Fairbanks physician Doctor Gillespie and Charlie Brower, the trader from Point Barrow. Brower told us that he had just certified for bounty leg bones of two coyotes from the Barrow area [the Territory paid a bounty on coyotes at the time, requiring leg bones for proof]. He said the northern Eskimos weren't familiar with coyotes.

I was at Barrow in 1950 and 1951 and asked some of the Eskimos about coyotes. They said that in 1939 and 1940 maybe half a dozen were taken along the arctic coast, but none since then.

Sheep use the lower mountain benches for lambing, and in late spring and summer they follow the snow line as it moves up. I've always thought they were after the new tender feed that comes out from under the snow. I've noticed too, that if a summer is dry and hot, during the fall hunting season sheep are found high in the mountains, as high as there is vegetation. I've had nonresident hunters comment that the wolves must have been after them because they were so high.

Sheep follow the snowline back down in the fall. A heavy snowfall in August can drive sheep down almost to the willows. But with a little south wind or a chinook to warm things and melt snow, they'll climb back into the hills. A good portion of sheep probably winter twenty or thirty miles from where they summer.

In late October the old rams run the tops of ridges trying to gather harems. Every so often I've seen a ram running up and down along the edge of ice on a mountain stream where he will decide the going might be better on the other side of the river.

I had learned to read some of the body language of sheep,

which is similar to that of caribou, moose, and other grazing animals. When a sheep raises its head high, becomes rigid, and, ears forward, stares fixedly at something, a wolf, a man, something different, it sends a message to other sheep; possible danger. The others behave similarly until the situation is resolved.

Sometimes when a sheep is concerned about an intruder, or is surprised by the sudden appearance of a man or wolf, it will stamp the ground with a front leg, and at the same time it may blow loudly through its nose.

Sheep are more alert to danger from below. It's much easier to stalk them from above.

Another interesting sheep habit became clear to me one day after I had spotted a ram I wanted. He was some distance from me across a treeless slope where there was no cover for a stalk. The lone ram, with a nice set of full curl horns, grazed four or five hundred yards from me. Between us was a low swale. He was too far for me to shoot, and I could see no way I could stalk closer without alarming him.

For some time I sprawled behind rocks watching the ram through my binoculars. It stopped feeding occasionally and looked toward me. I was sure it hadn't seen or scented me, and the behavior puzzled me. This continued for a good half an hour.

I was surprised when the ram stopped feeding and abruptly ran down a trail, through the low swale, and directly toward me. I shot him when he was within about fifty yards.

I've seen this behavior many times since; a sheep that stops feeding and frequently looks in one direction, is signaling where it intends to travel. Sometimes it makes its move by running, other times it continues to graze in that direction.

Sheep hunters should know that the ram with the biggest horns in a bunch is the leader. He'll be in the lead of a column of rams. If, while hunting, you see rams traveling single file, you can be sure the lead ram has the biggest horns.

Several old timers told me that Dall sheep can't swim, but I learned differently one late September when I made a solo hunt to get a ram for meat, which, in my view, is Alaska's tastiest and mildest. I wasn't looking for a trophy. Early in the morning I climbed a ridge

Four nice Dall rams taken on the Walter Holmes hunt of 1937. All appear to be full curl or better. Individual shown is Seebolt, a member of the Holmes party. ROSEMARIE OLSEN

where, from a distance, I had seen the white specks that were sheep. They were feeding in a green grass area below the snow line.

About noon I slipped up on three rams and killed the biggest. I dressed it as the old-time market hunters did when they packed sheep out of the mountains - I removed the guts, the head, and lower legs, and lashed the 120-pound carcass to my packboard, and started down.

I took my time, and stopped frequently to rest. Once I stopped about 100 yards above a good size stream in the valley below. As I rested, a full-curl ram appeared. He trotted along a trail that led to the river. He didn't see me, and I remained motionless. He stopped at the river's edge, and for a short time he paced back and forth, while peering across the river. It appeared he wanted to cross.

He finally made up his mind, and waded in. The river was rather swift, and he was quickly swept downstream. When he could no longer wade, he lunged as if making a jump, and he became almost submerged; about all that remained above water was his head and horns. He lunged again and again popped to the surface and made some progress, only to lunge and submerge again. He continued in this manner clear across the river.

It was almost as if he wasn't really swimming, but leaping through the water. With each lunge, he almost disappeared except for his head and horns. He would then surface. I guess his hollow hair brought him up. He must have pulled all four of his feet against his belly as he made each lunge.

Despite all his thrashing, progress was slow, and he was carried far downstream before he reached the far side.

I've seen sheep swimming in this manner several times since, and I've found tracks where a sheep entered a river, and found the tracks where it came out far downstream on the other side.

It's an odd way of swimming. The old timers were wrong; sheep do swim, if you want to call it that.

In October and November especially, sheep may cross from one mountain to another, and occasionally you'll see one in an unusual place, as one I once saw on Donnelly Dome [a small isolated dome found some miles north of the Alaska Range). They commonly move twenty or thirty miles between winter and summer range.

In fall, rams spread out, running the ridges, looking for ewes, and they may travel many miles. Breeding commences in late October and through much of November, at which time they fight over harems.

I had a perfect view one October of two rams as they fought high on an Alaska Range ridge. As a preliminary to the main event, they butted their horns together a few times from a standing position. Soon, it became more serious. Each walked a few steps from the other, and at what may have been a signal of some kind, each pivoted, poured on the coal, and they ran to slam their horns together.

This continued, and the distance between them before each meeting gradually increased. After five or six of these runs and violent slamming together, they were about twenty to thirty feet or so apart before they wheeled and ran at each other. The violent coming together of two roughly 250-pound rams running at full speed makes a terrible sound. You wonder how their skulls and necks stand it. I also wondered if it doesn't give them a headache.

Eventually, after a dozen or so violent meetings, one ram turned and kept going, perhaps planning to look for a ram with a softer head. The winner didn't chase him and didn't seem to hold anything against the loser.

Dall sheep winter kill if they are caught in deep snow with no wind to blow it clear; they cannot dig through deep snow for their feed. Many were killed in deep snow in Mount McKinley Park during the mid-1930s. Some were picked up in such bad shape that they were down with their hair frozen to the snow. In their weakened condition they couldn't get up.

For a time, the University of Alaska Experimental Farm at Fairbanks had some captive Dalls. They got awfully skinny during the first part of summer. It seemed that the heat and flies were very bothersome to them. A few died from pneumonia. The altitude of the University farm was probably too low, and the climate may have been too damp, for them. They probably didn't have to use the lung capacity they normally would while living high in the mountains.

The university experimented in crossing the Dalls with domestic sheep. One crossbred ram in particular that resulted was a big wild-eyed critter with hollow wavy hair with kind of a curl to it. He had a wonderful set of horns. He looked like a pure Dall, except for the curly hair. At the age of six, he had horns that a wild sheep might attain at nine or ten years.

Rika Wallen, who ran a roadhouse near Big Delta, had a small flock of domestic sheep. She arranged with the University to borrow the wavy-haired ram, hoping he would breed with her ewes which had been without a ram for some years. Unfortunately, her ewes acted like a bunch of old maids—they were scared of the big ram. He had plenty of ambition, but it takes two to tango, and no lambs resulted from the attempted crossing.

Twins are uncommon with Dall sheep; perhaps one ewe of every ten or fifteen will drop twins in the spring. However, it is rare to see twin lambs in the fall. I think it is survival of the fittest;

one lamb is usually stronger than the other, gets more food, and perhaps more protection from its mother. The other simply doesn't make it. Nature never favors a weakling.

In my thirty years of observing sheep, I've seen perhaps twenty-five sets of twins in the fall.

I think eagles are hard on newborn lambs. Once, after I had taken my pack string with a load of freight to a mine high in the Alaska Range, on my return trip I took a short cut over a high bald ridge—an easy climb for the horses without loads. As I topped that ridge I looked down a few hundred feet to see eight or ten ewes, each with a lamb. I kept the horses out of sight, and sat to watch. The agile white lambs, probably not over a week old, chased each other, zigzagging among the ewes, leaped on top of rocks, and leaped off. They butted one another, and one even jumped on top of and walked around on, a bedded ewe—probably its mother. From time to time lambs nursed, always from the side or rear. All wild babies are attractive; pure white Dall sheep are especially appealing.

While the lambs played, the ewes fed or were bedded down, seeming to enjoy the midday sun.

There was a sudden change. A ewe leaped to her feet. She must have called, for her lamb rushed to her. She stood with the lamb directly under her body. The other ewes followed the same routine. I was puzzled until I saw an eagle circling above the little flock.

The eagle selected a ewe and lamb that were somewhat apart from the others. It stooped on the ewe with its claws outstretched. It didn't hit the ewe, but came close enough to have raked it with its talons. It climbed with powerful wing strokes, circled, and again folded wings and stooped at the same ewe and lamb.

While the attacks took place, every lamb was sheltered under the belly of its mother. Every ewe's eyes followed the eagle's flight. The eagle again came so close it could have raked the ewe. For a third time the big bird flapped for altitude, circled and stooped. This time the targeted ewe leaped and struck at it with her horns. She missed.

My sympathy was with the sheep. When the eagle again climbed and circled, it passed directly over me at about 100 feet. It was flying into the wind, and it was moving slowly relative to the ground. I didn't even have to lead it. I snapped a shot with my .30-06. Feathers flew, and it collapsed. The wind carried it back, and the bloody bundle of feathers nearly landed on one of my horses on the back side of the ridge. The sound of the shot, and the dead eagle thumping on the ground, spooked my horses and the sheep.

The sheep ran off. I calmed the horses, and continued on my way with a mild feeling of accomplishment.

Chasing Moose

IN 1926, I WAS A CHEECHAKO (newcomer to Alaska) when I had a very close call with a moose. Elmer Nelson, who came into the country with me, and I, lived at Miller Roadhouse, on the Richardson Highway, twenty-two miles from where I later built my Summit Lake Lodge. Moose were scarce. Whenever we saw one, if possible we killed it.

Elmer and I saw a mulligan bull (young, with small antlers) standing facing us. At first it looked like a man standing and wearing a big hat. It was perhaps 300 yards off, but it looked so big we thought we could hit it. After we fired a few shots, it limped into the brush.

In later years, I learned that a wounded moose will often head for water, if a stream, pond, or lake is near.

Dark was near, but we trailed him to where he had crossed the Gulkana river, where we had to quit for the day. At daylight next morning, wearing hip boots, we crossed the river and picked up his tracks on the far side. We saw a little blood with the tracks, and trailed him for about a quarter of a mile and found him bedded down.

He didn't move as we approached, and I thought he was dead. His head was up, but it looked as if his eyes were closed. I walked up and kicked a hind foot.

He exploded straight up. That was the most moose I have ever

Slim stood six feet tall; the moose rack he is holding approaches a spread of 60 inches. It's probably from an old bull past his prime, judging by the short length of the tines projecting from the palms.
Rosemarie Olsen

seen so close. I couldn't raise my rifle because he was in the way, not that it would have done any good; I didn't have a shell in the chamber. I tried to run backward.

Elmer was about six feet to one side of the moose. As it leaped out of its bed, he stuck his rifle against its head and pulled the trigger. The moose collapsed. I was still staggering back. I tripped on a root and landed on my rear, still holding my unloaded rifle.

It happened in seconds, and I felt like a fool. It was a valuable lesson. I've never been careless in approaching a downed animal, especially a moose, since.

One of our bullets had hit a hind leg below the knee. I've since noticed that a wounded moose seldom goes far before it beds down.

I had a strangely similar experience with a big bull moose in the fall of 1950. I was guiding a nonresident hunter after moose, and late one day we saw a nice bull accompanied by a cow. It was too late in the day to go after them. "They'll be here in the morning. We'll get up early and go after them," I said.

Shortly after daylight I spotted the bull's antlers sticking out of the brush, where he was bedded. We got within 200 yards. I grunted a few times, and he stood.

The hunter emptied his rifle at him. With his last shot, the bull dropped. He was on a steep slope, in very dense brush. I went above where the bull had dropped, and worked down to him.

I found him floating on brush; no part of his body was touching ground. His feet were uphill. He was breathing, so I threw a shell into the barrel as I neared.

I told the hunter, who had followed me. "It's going to be a tough job gutting him here. This brush is really thick."

I wasn't sure of the moose's condition. He was absolutely still, but breathing. Wary, and from a safe distance, while standing on willows, I kicked one of his extended legs.

He exploded into violent kicking. His body settled. He rolled clear over; his feet had been uphill, but the violence of his kicking rolled him so his feet were now on the downhill side. By then he was twenty feet or so from me, and the willows were so high and dense I could scarcely see him. He got to his feet and I heard him tearing away through the willows as though he was unhurt. The hunter was in thick brush and couldn't see him.

I fought through the brush to the nearest opening and saw the moose, on a long trot, at about seventy-five yards. He was traveling like he had never been hit. When he was as far as I cared for a supposedly crippled moose to get, I fired once and broke his neck.

While dressing him, I found the hunter's bullet had partly cut the big sinew that controlled his head. The shock knocked him down and out. He dropped as if it were a killing shot.

He was climbing when hit. He rolled backward and landed on his back in the brush, legs uphill, as I found him.

A moose's long powerful legs can be dangerous. I've seen them kick when in death throes after being shot. They may throw a hind leg up close to their head and kick it back. I'm always careful to never get near; anyone caught by such a kick could be badly hurt.

Also, those hoofs are sharp. Years ago I mined at Slate Creek in the Alaska Range, about twenty-five miles east of the Richardson Highway, and I used dogs to help me pack supplies to the mine. One fall day I was headed for the mine with several pack-carrying dogs. Walking down a hill I saw a bull moose in a pond at the bottom. He saw us and waded ashore. The dogs saw him and broke, despite my yells. One caught up to the moose at the edge of the lake.

The moose jumped on that dog. All four legs worked like pistons, as he danced. His sharp hoofs sliced like knives. He made hamburger and a dead dog in nothing flat.

A moose is nothing to toy with; it's big and powerful. Car collisions with moose have killed or injured a lot of Alaskans. Also, a moose can put you in trouble in surprising ways. In the early 1950s three hunters I knew were in a small riverboat drifting down the Salcha River looking for a moose. They passed the mouth of a slough and saw a bull moose feeding there. Jesse Davis, the boat owner, turned the boat toward the moose, and one of the others started to shoot it.

"Don't shoot. Wait until I can beach us," Davis called.

The moose had just gotten his front feet on the bank to climb out of the water when one of the men shot it. It dropped back in the water, and half sank. They pulled the boat near, and it floated over the moose's legs. They threw the painter over the antlers, planning to tow the moose to a nearby gravel bar.

As they started to tow, the moose came to, and started to kick the bottom of the boat. The boat rock so violently that the men were nearly tossed overboard.

The moose got out from under the boat, made his feet, got ashore, and charged up the bank. The painter was still looped on his antlers. He towed the boat as if it were a toy.

Davis grabbed his rifle, and, despite being slammed around by the traveling boat, shot the moose in the stern, dropping him.

The shot spoiled a lot of good meat. When the other two guys gave him hell for it, he told them, "That's my boat the moose was starting to drag across country."

Moose often become cranky during deep snow months. One March, my wife Margaret and I were looking at beaver houses from a bank of the Delta River. Snow was drifted pretty deep, and in places it was ten or twelve feet down to the water. We had run into a couple of cows with their calves. I had an ice chisel, Margaret a shovel. I beat on the chisel with pliers, and that put the run on them with no problem.

Then we ran into a big bull. He either had to go into deep snow at the edge of the woods, or return our way. When a moose gets angry, it brings its lips together real fast, and runs its tongue out and up his nostrils. Its hair pitches forward.

This guy didn't want to go into deep snow. As I beat the chisel with pliers, he quickly turned around. Then he turned back and looked at us. His ears were laid back tight against his head, his hair was all forward. His tongue was out, lips smacking.

"That's close enough," he was telling us.

We weren't carrying a gun.

"I think we'd better walk a circle around this guy," I suggested.

"You can stand there if you want to. I'm already walking one," Margaret said. I followed her, and the bull, which had gotten his way, relaxed, and stood watching us.

If you walk between a moose calf that has been cached by its mother, you're in trouble right now. That old lady is dangerous until the calf is about a month old, when it is capable of following her.

Art Smith, a pilot who often worked with me on hunts, and Chuck Taylor, from Fairbanks, were with me while hunting brown bears on the Alaska Peninsula. They were hunting near Little Mother Goose Lake, which lies in a canyon about a mile and a half above Mother Goose Lake. A cow moose, with ears laid back, frantically charged them. She had a big, raw torn place on her shoulder, probably made by a bear.

She ran tight circles around and around the hunters. They didn't want to shoot her, and stood back-to-back, rifles ready if she actually attacked. She ran so fast they almost became dizzy trying to turn with her.

That old girl circled them at least fifteen times, each time a bit closer. She was almost lying over on her side as she turned. She ran off a ways, and returned, to run around them again. A time or two she was almost close enough to touch. She finally left, her hair still on end, still on the prod.

Next day they saw a brown bear chasing the same moose – the torn side identified her. They killed the brownie. They figured a brownie had probably killed her calf, putting her on the peck.

During the late 1920s and 1930s moose were scarce in the country around my cabin at Summit Lake. For seven or eight years I trapped the adjacent upper Delta and Tangle Lake country, and never saw a moose track during winter. A moose or two would usually go through in the fall. I always packed a rifle, and when I saw tracks of a moose, I'd take off after it. Sometimes the only way I could get a moose was to go over on the Gakona River, and even then I didn't always get one.

About 1932 or 1933 I was trapping out of my camp near Paxson, about ten miles from where I built Summit Lake Lodge. One day in late November, while driving my dog team, I saw fresh tracks of a moose where it had crossed the Richardson Highway near One-Mile Creek. I hadn't killed a moose that fall, and there were no caribou around. I needed meat.

The moose had fed his way up the creek. I was pretty sure the tracks were made by a bull. A bull's tracks spread, especially in fall during the rut. He seems to spread his toes more and more until it almost gets like he is going to break them. A cow keeps her toes together. I think there are scent glands between bull moose toes.

I turned the dogs around, drove to camp, unhooked and tied them, and, on snowshoes, took to the moose's trail. I didn't take a pack.

I cut over a hill and picked up his tracks. He'd go this way and that, and he worked his way up into the timber behind Paxson roadhouse. I figure he got my wind. I didn't see him, but I found where he'd started trotting east toward ten-mile-distant Gakona River.

I returned to my camp, spent the night, and got up before daylight next morning to follow that moose. I thought I knew where he'd go on the Gakona. There's a big willow flat back of Fish Lake, about half way to the Gakona, and moose often hang out there. I took a pack with a little grub and a saw, and on snowshoes, headed out. I went without blankets, figuring if I had to stay out overnight I could always build a fire.

When I broke over into the Gakona valley, the tracks went south, down river, instead of up as I had expected. I stayed on that moose's trail all day, and routed him out several times, but he was always in the timber, and I didn't get a glimpse of him.

When it began to get dark, I picked a place where I could cut a lot of dry brush and went to work with the saw. I siwashed and fed a fire all night. I didn't get much sleep.

When it was light enough to travel next morning, I took after him again. He had followed the Gakona River down about eight miles, crossed it, and started upstream on the other side. About one o'clock in the afternoon I caught up with him where he was feeding in a little willow patch. I topped a little ridge and there he was, within easy range. One shot did the job.

I dressed, skinned, and quartered him. By then it was dark. One can always see 4,600-foot Wolverine Mountain, about four miles from Paxson, and I headed straight over the hills toward it. I arrived at my camp at one o'clock in the morning. In two days I had snowshoed about forty miles.

My dogs had gone a day without food, and I'd lost a night of sleep, but I had a moose out of the deal. I slept in the next morning, and relaxed all day. The following day I retrieved the meat with my dog team.

Today (1956) moose numbers have rebuilt. I could start walking from here (Summit Lake Lodge) and could kill a moose every day of the season, with no better equipment than I had when I trailed that moose into the Gakona nearly twenty-five years ago.

Market hunting, which ended in 1925, knocked moose numbers

Slim with Cecelia ("Butch") Neuweiler, a resident of Pennsylvania, who usually accompanied her husband Phil on his big game hunts. Butch was a fine rifle shot, and an experienced big game hunter. This bull, still in the velvet, was probably close to his prime, judging from the length of antler tines. Photo taken in 1962. ROSEMARIE OLSEN

down. It was largely a winter activity, when bull moose are poor eating, so the market hunters preferred to kill cow moose. There were also a number of Indians roaming the country in summer, living from the land. They had to hunt, for there was no work for Natives in those years. They didn't hunt because they liked to hunt; they hunted because it was necessary if they were going to eat.

Natives I knew believed that meat of an unborn or newborn moose calf was a cure for almost any disease. They called it "soft meat." In 1927, relatives of patients at the hospital at Fort Yukon were bringing to patients much meat of unborn moose calves. Sam O. White, the game warden there, made a deal with the hospital authorities. If they caught an Indian bringing unborn calf meat to anyone in the hospital, that ended his visiting privilege. That rule saved a lot of cow moose, and their calves. At the same time, Sam enforced the new (1925) Alaska Game Commission's regulations that allowed hunters to kill bulls only.

As times changed and the country where it was burned (many old-timers, and Natives, deliberately set forest fires to clear brush, to make travel easier, and to ease mineral prospecting and mining), began to put up new growth, market hunting ended, the Indians found jobs, and moose have made a great comeback.

5
Chasing Griz Over a Mountain

AUTHOR: THROUGH MUCH OF THE EARLY 20TH CENTURY, Alaska's bears were considered pests by most bush residents. They wrecked camps and cabins, attacked and frightened horses (there were few cars or trucks), and occasionally mauled, and sometimes killed people. Owners of bush cabins commonly built pole caches to protect food and other items, mostly from bears.

In 1911, Alaska's governor Walter Clark asked for a twelve month open season on bears. "They are dangerous animals," he proclaimed. In 1915, Governor John Strong said that, "Unless the Kodiak brown bear can be practically exterminated, cattle and sheep raising in Alaska will probably be abandoned."

As late as the 1950s, a federal fishery biologist recommended killing Kodiak brown bears because he thought they were catching too many spawning salmon from a tributary stream at Karluk Lake.

During the late 1920s and early 1930s, grizzly bears were abundant in the Alaska Range, where Slim Moore lived. So abundant, that, in May, 1922, Frank Glaser (my book *Alaska's Wolf Man; The 1915–1955 Wilderness Adventures of Frank Glaser*) in only ten days of hunting, killed seventeen of them near the site of the old Yost Roadhouse, seventeen miles south of Paxson's. Glaser collected these grizzlies as scientific specimens at the request of Dr. E. W. Nelson of the U.S. Biological Survey.

For killing those bears, Glaser was repeatedly thanked by

Alaska Road Commission workers and teamsters who drove horses on what was then a wagon trail between Valdez and Fairbanks, and is now the Richardson Highway. A few Model T Ford drivers who used the old trail also thanked Glaser. To all of these, the abundant grizzly bears were dangerous pests, and to them it was good riddance.

Alaska's bear world has changed. Modern Alaskans treasure their bears. Grizzly, brown, and black bears, in compliance with the state constitution, are scientifically managed for sustained production. Many residents of Anchorage, Alaska's largest city, take pride in having both grizzly and black bears living within the city limits. Some citizens get upset when any of these urban bears are killed for safety reasons.

During the 1940s there was no bag limit in Alaska for brown and grizzly bears. By 1950, the bag limit was two bears a season. In 1969 the bag limit was set at one every four years, which, with minor exceptions, is the current regulation.

Today, brown, grizzly and black bears are found in healthy numbers generally throughout Alaska, with open hunting seasons and bag limits appropriate for each of the twenty-six game management units.

SLIM: I had a dog team in the late 1920s and early 1930s, and, like all dog team owners, I was always looking for food for them. Sled dogs like bear meat, and grizzly bears were abundant along the Richardson Highway where it transected the Alaska Range past Paxson's roadhouse, and Summit Lake, where I lived. At the time, most bush residents considered these bears to be undesirable pests.

One October day in the early 1930s, when there was a few inches of snow on the ground and the temperature was around ten above, I slipped on knee-high mukluks, shrugged into my parka, and left my cabin to see if I could get a bear. A day or two earlier, a neighbor from ten miles down the graveled Richardson Highway had seen fresh grizzly tracks near the Gulkana River. Most bears had gone into hibernation by then.

Slim skinning a bear in 1937. Smoky fire was probably a deterrent for mosquitoes. ROSEMARIE OLSEN

I thought it would be nice to have an attractive grizzly skin, and I could use the bear meat to feed my dog team.

I followed the Gulkana River downstream from Paxson's Roadhouse, to where my neighbor had seen the tracks, and soon located fresh grizzly tracks in new snow. A cold spell had formed ice on the river here and there, but there was still much open water in which I saw a few late spawning salmon. Water in the Gulkana was perfectly clear, and I could almost count the scales on the fish, most of which had turned red, normal spawning color.

Bear tracks and salmon remnants along the shoreline told the story; at least one grizzly had recently been fishing there. I slipped along, peering through willows, hoping to find the fishing bear. I had sneaked about three hundred yards in this manner when, ahead, I heard branches breaking as an animal I assumed to be a bear fled. It had probably winded me and knew enough to take off.

I rushed into the open, yanked mittens off, and prepared to shoot. I didn't see him until he was about 200 yards off, walking on the edge of a deep gully. He was a large bear, with a cream-colored body, and brownish legs.

I aimed at his shoulder, allowing a bit for bullet drop, and fired my .30-06. He reared as if hit, and dropped into the gulley.

I thought I had killed him. A client had recently given me some 220-grain Peters ammunition which I had fed into my rifle for the bear hunt. My rifle was sighted for 180-grain ammo. The change to heavier bullets caused me to hit low. I didn't know it until later, but the bullet punched a hole in the muscle of the bear's front leg, and cut a groove across his brisket.

When I reached the gulley's steep rim, in the bottom I saw a fair amount of blood and a big hole in the snow where he had fallen. His trail in the snow was clear, and I took off after him, thinking he was badly wounded. "He can't go far," I told myself. I was without snowshoes, for there was only a few inches of snow on that level, and I hadn't planned on a long hunt.

"Never allow an animal you have wounded escape to die a lingering death," was a maxim I learned as a boy, and I have always tried to live by it.

He fled to the top of 5,226-foot-high Paxson Mountain. By then I had doubts that he was seriously wounded. Wading in knee-deep snow that had fallen at this altitude, I stuck to his trail. I became warm while climbing and kept my speed below the sweating stage; cold weather and sweat-dampened clothing can be deadly.

I thought the bear would weaken from loss of blood, but the farther he traveled, the less blood I found.

The bear and I topped Paxson Mountain. Despite an icy wind at that altitude, I enjoyed the snowy panorama from there. Towering peaks of the Alaska Range surrounded me, and I could see the rich lowland valley of Maclaren River leading off into the distance beyond the Tangle Lakes country, where the bear seemed to be headed.

I soon spotted him about 500 yards below me, still trudging along steadily. He was a tiny target, but it was my first sight of him since I had fired my first shot. I had to try a few shots. I held well above him, guessing where because I didn't normally shoot at anything at that range, and fired several times. One bullet hit him in the heel of a hind foot, breaking his ankle.

He kept going. Sometimes the damaged foot stepped naturally, other times it turned. That slowed him, and I began to gain.

After we left Paxson Mountain, I saw him walk into a deep draw. I knew he'd stay in the bottom to keep under cover. The draw made a big bend, and, I ran across it to cut him off.

My timing was perfect; when I reached the draw he was within 100 yards, directly below me.

"Where do you think you're going now?" I hollered at him.

He turned, snarled, and charged. I waited until he was within twenty-five yards and shot him down through the hump, killing him instantly.

I then discovered where my bullets had hit, and suddenly realized why. I felt pretty foolish. If I had used my usual 180 grain bullets, which my rifle was sighted for, I'd have hit him about a foot higher with my first shot, and likely killed him.

It was late in the day, near dark, and I was fourteen miles from where I had picked up his trail. The temperature was close to zero.

I quickly skinned him, warming my bare hands on his body from time to time as the cold bit. He seemed a bit lean for a fall bear, which may have explained his October fishing effort.

I left the head and feet unskinned. His hide squared (average of length and width) a little over eight feet—a very big bear for Alaska's Interior. Few grizzlies were killed by sportsmen in those years. Most hunters sought moose, caribou, or sheep, for they were after meat. As a result, there were many big old grizzlies wandering the country.

I finished skinning in the dark, and dragged the skin downhill to a stand of scattered spruce trees. I stretched the skin out on a level spot, fur side up, and brushed the snow from it. I was very tired, and his fur felt like a cozy feather bed when I crawled onto it. I used the head for a pillow, and threw the feet across my body. The weight of the feet still in the skin held it in place. It made a nice blanket, although it didn't smell like roses; the aroma was that of the fish upon which he had been feeding.

I wore heavy wool underwear, plus my parka, and inside the richly furred bear skin I was soon warm. I fell into a wonderful sleep, but occasionally awoke because of my unusual situation.

The sky was clear and it was calm. A full moon arose, yellow at first, then, as it sailed higher, it became silvery. With the clean snow, the world about me seemed almost as bright as daylight. Nearby snowflakes on the ground twinkled like diamonds from the moonglow. The land was dead silent. It was almost surreal, as I lay warm inside that grizzly skin, gazing at the big round silvery moon, jillions of stars, and an occasional burst of green and red dancing northern lights.

Around one or two in the morning, for ten or fifteen minutes a couple of wolves howled from a few hundred yards away. I enjoyed their serenade, and wondered if they were aware of my presence. I dozed, and when I again awoke, I heard an animal slowly walking nearby, breaking the light snow crust.

"Surely a wolf wouldn't come here, with human and grizzly scent all around," I thought, as I remained motionless, waiting.

My rifle was handy inside the bear skin. When I figured the critter was as close as it would likely come, I threw my arms up, kicked my feet to throw the bear skin apart, and sat up, rifle ready. I was astonished to see a porcupine about fifteen feet away. He too was surprised, and wheeled his rear toward me and started flipping his tail, as porkies do when faced with danger.

The porky went on his way in peace, and I pulled the bear skin back around me and slept peacefully for the remainder of the night. Frozen bear skin is limber like frozen bacon; it doesn't become overly hard, so the frozen skin didn't trap me.

Next day I rolled the skin and cached it high in a tree, and started for home. I didn't want to climb Paxson mountain again, so I went around it, a much longer walk. I hadn't eaten anything since the morning of the previous day, and was pretty near starved. The fishy bear meat hadn't tempted me, but I kicked myself for not shooting the porcupine for food, although its meat rates pretty low on my menu.

I decided if I ran into anything edible I would shoot and eat it.

It was a long slog home. I arrived at little Mud Lake [which today is near the east end of today's Denali Highway]. Near dark I found a flock of spruce grouse perched in a nearby tree. With my .30-06 I shot the heads off of two of them, built a fire, and roasted and ate every bit of both.

I arrived at my cabin long after dark, and learned a search was planned for me. On the day I went hunting, I was supposed to have had dinner ready for two fellows who had planned to spend the night with me. When I didn't return home, they picked up my tracks in the snow and followed them to where I'd started up Paxson Mountain. That turned them back. They were older than me, and the mountain was more than they wanted to tackle.

That November, near trapping season, accompanied by old timer Frank Panning, I drove my dog team to where I'd left the bear carcass. Frank and I both trapped in that country.

Snow was falling, with a strong wind. It was about fifteen above. Near where I had left the bear carcass, I asked Frank to wait and to watch my dogs while I checked things out. I learned early in my time in Alaska to be wary when approaching a kill of any kind.

On snowshoes, I climbed to within about fifty yards of the carcass. Through falling snow I saw something partly covered by snow lying near it. A bit of fur showed, and I thought it might be another bear. About then, I patted myself on the back for being cautious. Grizzlies do eat grizzlies, and a grizzly is occasionally found out of its den during winter.

I was downhill from the carcass, not a good place to be if a bear was lying there. I removed my mittens and readied my rifle (with 180 grain bullets) as I stomped around trying to gain elevation, peering, and edging closer, trying to see what was half-buried next to the carcass.

A camp robber (northern jay) landed on the carcass. A wolf leaped out of the snow and snapped at it. He missed, and the jay flew off. My rifle leaped to my shoulder, I aimed, fired, and the wolf dropped.

At my shot, to my amazement, snow around the carcass exploded as five more wolves that had been sleeping there jumped into sight. They scrambled all directions.

One ran toward me, saw me, and veered. I ignored it. As the

others fled, I fired five times, each time yank-slamming the bolt, and firing again. I connected three times, watching with delight as three wolves plowed their noses into the snow and rolled to a stop.

With the rifle empty, I hastily pushed a cartridge into the barrel, swung around, and at about a hundred and fifty yards, killed the one that had sped past me. As my bullet struck him, he pinwheeled in a great shower of snow and lay quiet.

I had killed five of the six wolves that had been bedded near the bear carcass. Four of those wolves had been in a perfect line. If I'd known that, I could have killed all four with one shot. I'll never get another chance like that.

The Territory paid a twenty dollar bounty on wolves. The wolf skins brought a nice price as well. A working man's day wages was about five bucks, so I was well paid for my two-day bear hunt across Paxson Mountain. I also had a beautiful bear skin which warmed my feet mornings when I rolled out of bed.

The frozen bear carcass had kept well. Forty or fifty pounds had been eaten by wolves. My sled dogs ate the rest.

6
A Bare-handed Encounter with a Wolf

AUTHOR: DURING SLIM MOORE'S TIME in Alaska, wolves were looked upon as "bad" animals. They killed moose, caribou, sheep, and other animals prized by residents. Through the 1950s, the federal government's policy was to kill wolves wherever they were found. From the 1920s through the 1950s the Territory paid a bounty for a wolf ($20 early, $50 in later years).

Alaskans generally supported this war on wolves.

Through the 1950's, until statehood, federal wildlife agents, using shotguns, killed wolves from small planes; full-time predator agents poisoned wolves by dropping strychnine baits from airplanes, and by injecting poison into carcasses of caribou and other animals they killed for the purpose. A contrivance called a "coyote getter" was widely used; when a wolf (or any other animal) picked up a scented tuft of wool, a trigger fired a lethal poison into the animal's mouth.

Alaska, as a state, assumed management of its fish and game in 1960. The wolf was immediately classified both as a big game animal and a furbearer—the only animal with dual classification. Poison of any kind was banned. Bag limits and closed seasons for wolves were established, varying with the twenty-six game management units. The wolf bounty was dropped in 1970. Alaska's constitution requires that replenishable resources be utilized, developed, and maintained on the sustained yield principle, and that includes the wolf.

The public's attitude on wolves, nationally, and also in Alaska, has changed 180 degrees; now the wolf is regarded by most as the primary representative of wilderness; it is a much-loved totem.

With statehood, Alaska's wolves, which are prolific, soon recovered their original abundance. There are around 10,000 wolves in Alaska today, of which trappers and hunters annually harvest roughly 1,000. At times wolves, an efficient predator, threaten populations of moose, caribou, and other valuable species. Again, the state constitution requires that renewable resources, which, of course, include moose, caribou, sheep, and other prey species, must be managed on the sustained yield basis.

When wolves seriously threaten a prey population, to protect whatever prey species is involved, the Alaska Board of Game may decide to reduce (not eliminate) wolf numbers. A goal is set by the Board for the number of wolves that need to be removed. This is beneficial to both wolves (it is difficult for many to understand this) and their prey.

Wolves are capable of wiping out their prey within a region, thus eliminating their own food source, which forces a reduction in their own population. Historians have has recorded times when both wolves and their prey were rare in areas of Alaska, most likely a result of wolf predation.

When wolf numbers need to be reduced, it is accomplished by shooting them from small planes. This is not "hunting," as opponents to wolf control claim. It is control. At no time since statehood has the goal ever been to remove all wolves from an area. Qualified wildlife biologists make recommendations to the Board of Game for this work, and they oversee and regularly report on results.

Thus, Slim Moore viewed wolves as "bad" animals during his years afield. It was then the view of most Alaskans, as well as the official federal and territorial position.

Slim: I've trapped quite a few wolves, and shot a few. The craziest mixup I ever had with a wolf was at Paxson Lake about 1935. A wolf had stepped into one of my traps, broke the chain, and got away with the trap. A week or so later I went to check some of my other traps. I carried an old .30-30 lever action rifle that day, having left my .30-06 at another cabin.

According to Slim, the wolf is by far the smartest animal in Alaska, and the most difficult to trap of any fur animal. Alaska's wolves vary in color from near-white, to solid black. This gray wolf is probably the most common color. ALASKA DEPARTMENT OF FISH AND GAME

When I got almost to Paxson Lake, I picked up a wolf track. I thought he was dragging the trap, and the tracks looked as though he was running. I followed the tracks to the edge of the lake and saw the wolf, a black, on the lake ice. He was 250 or 300 yards from me, too far for certain shooting with the .30-30. I held my sights well above him, and pitched a few shots at him anyway. As he went into the brush at the lake's edge, my third shot appeared to upend it.

I was on snowshoes, and ran across the lake and into the brush after him. I saw a few drops of blood in his tracks. That convinced me I had made a solid hit. From my earliest years I had been taught that when an animal is wounded, I was to make every effort to finish it; I've always hated the idea of having an animal I wounded suffer a painful, lingering death.

The .30-30 was old when I got it second hand, and I hadn't used it much. It had been around my cabin for several years. After the shot that appeared to upend the wolf, I jacked a fresh shell in, and the rifle jammed. I later found I had mixed a .32 Special shell with the others, and I couldn't get it out, or in.

I was fairly certain the wolf was hard hit, and was only going a short distance, so I continued to run after him. From the lake, he ran into loose snow that was a good four feet deep. That slowed him, and I gained. When I neared him, he was almost out of sight, lunging and fighting the deep, loose snow. In a way, he was kind of breaking trail for me.

He realized he'd made a mistake by going into the loose snow, and tried to turn back toward the lake where he could run on ice. However, I was between him and the lake, and every time he tried to turn, I cut him off.

While on the run, I broke off a ten-foot-high dead snag, a gee-pole spruce, planning to use it as a club. I was close to the wolf, and he started to duck into patches of brush and under little spruce trees, trying to hide. Each time, I poked him out with the pole, and he ran on. I followed as fast as I could.

Finally, I poked him out from under a little brushy spruce tree. It was about 100 feet to the next little spruce. When he started for that one, I poured it on, giving it everything I had. I gained a little, because he was still handicapped by having to lunge through loose snow. When he was half way to the little tree I screamed, trying to fluster him.

It worked.

He stopped and turned, growling, and suddenly I was on him. Still running, I rapped him across the back with the spruce pole. It broke in two. I dropped the half I held, and climbed on him with my snowshoes.

He struggled violently to get out from under me. I almost invented a new dance step trying to stay balanced atop that struggling wolf. Both of us were handicapped by the deep loose snow; he more than me.

His head came up between my snowshoes. His mouth was

wide open. He snapped at my snowshoes, and tried to reach my feet and legs. All I had to work with was the jammed rifle.

I shoved the barrel into his open mouth, and kept shoving and twisting and shoving and twisting. The rifle barrel and front sight reached and tore his lungs. Soon blood poured from his mouth. He died quickly.

I dragged him back to the lake where I looked him over, and sat to rest. My bullet hadn't touched him. He had been bleeding slightly from what was probably an ice-cut on one foot. Other than that, he didn't have a scratch on him. I had run down and killed a healthy wolf.

I broke into a cold sweat when I realized that. Things could easily have gone another way; a wolf is a powerful, quick, and lethal predator. I would hate to try to fight one barehanded (or with a jammed .30-30) on solid ground; I'm not sure who would win.

He was a mature adult that weighed about eighty pounds [Author: Alaska's wolves average from eighty to 100 pounds]. I had chased him through loose snow for about a quarter of a mile from the lake edge. He had $20 that belonged to me (the Territorial bounty) and I wanted it, and his hide, for which I could also get a nice check. However, if I'd known he didn't have a trap on him, or that he wasn't hit, I wouldn't have been so anxious to climb on him.

Some wolves become giants: The biggest one I have ever seen had been feeding on a bear carcass I had shot. I caught the wolf there, and shot it too. It was so fat it looked like a seal when I removed its skin. I hung it on my scale and threw the skin back across it. That wolf weighed 140 pounds. The skin was eight-feet-four-inches long, and a foot wide—and it wasn't stretched. It was probably four or five-years old. I can't imagine having a bare-handed fight with such a huge brute.

Fairbanks-based Game Warden Sam White claimed I was the only man he knew who had ever killed a wolf with bare hands. As he told the story, when I got through wrestling the wolf I had hold of both ends of my .30-30.

Not true; I had hold of only one end of that old rifle.

Most captive wolves never become tame. They usually want to sneak off. However, I did see a tame one raised from a pup by "Butch" Henry Stock. Either Butch dug it out of a den, or Theo Van Bibber, who ran a dog livery in Fairbanks, may have given it to him.

It always ran loose, and from the time it was a pup, it slept on Butch's bed with him.

When it was about a year and a half old, Butch also had two dogs. For the fun of it, Butch occasionally took the dogs and the wolf out to watch them chase moose. He got a big kick out of seeing them run moose across country.

One winter the wolf stepped into one of Butch's traps, and spent the night there. Butch told me he mashed the spring down, and the wolf stepped out of it without biting or acting in any way hostile. It did lose a couple of toes.

Old Butch and the wolf made a good pair. He acquired his nickname when he arrived at Valdez with a small herd of cattle which he drove to Fairbanks and butchered. Over the years he was a gold miner, and at one time he owned two roadhouses.

Butch couldn't read or write. No one could live in a cabin that Butch used for any length of time. He never washed a dish or swept a floor. He piled garbage in a corner. He seldom changed clothing. He didn't care whether he had bedding, commonly sleeping in his clothes. When hunting, he took no bedding, but slept next to a fire at night even in below freezing temperature. He was one tough hombre.

Butch's wolf didn't last long. In the spring when it was two years old, when Rika Wallen, the lady owner of a roadhouse near Delta Junction, turned her sheep out, the wolf chased them a bit. Rika laid the law down to Butch, telling him what would happen to him if the wolf killed any of her sheep. Butch didn't dare buck Rika, who was prominent and respected.

He had the wolf shot.

Barney Dawson, who lived not far from my place on Summit Lake, boarded my sled dogs summers. He once raised some half-breed wolf pups. Once when I went to pick up my dogs, his half-breed wolves swam the Gulkana River, howled all evening, and remained on the far side as long as I was there. Their mother was a Russian wolf hound, and their father was a wolf. With that kind of breeding, I'd guess they hated themselves. I don't think those wolf-dogs ever amounted to much as sled dogs. I suspect they were too wild, and too hard to handle.

The wolf is by far the smartest animal in Alaska. If any animal is capable of thinking, it is the wolf. They'll commonly run a moose or a caribou to their favorite place to pull it down. I've found wolf-killed moose and back-tracked to see how the wolves managed to make their kill. They cooperate with one another. One will lie in ambush, while others drive the prey to it.

Wolves don't always win. I once saw tracks where wolves chased a moose on a willow flat where the going was pretty good, with solid footing. There was a lot of blood and a confusion of tracks. The moose spent a lot of time turning around and around, fending wolves off. He managed to make it into heavy timber where snow was deep and loose. The wolves quit there. They would have almost have had to swim, so deep was the snow. The moose could handle that, the wolves couldn't.

One winter I was looking after some horses that were loose and ranging near Jarvis Creek. I drove my dog team there about every day with a sack of oats. Wherever I'd find a horse, I'd pour him some oats and go on to find the others.

Near the mouth of the Jarvis, where it runs into the Delta River, I found where wolves had killed a cow moose the previous night. Tracks showed where two wolves had run her out of the timber. When the moose came to the Jarvis Creek bar, one wolf had short cut it and turned it, forcing it onto the ice of the Delta, where they killed it. Moose are almost helpless on slick ice; wolves can handle it pretty well. Those two wolves had their attack all planned.

WOLVES ARE THE MOST DIFFICULT TO TRAP of any fur animal. The best set I ever made for wolves was on bare windswept ridges where they like to run. I dug a hole in the fall, close to the side of a rock or something that was a natural wolf scent post. I'd drive a twelve-inch (120 penny) spike into the ground, with the trap chain fastened to it, and allow it to freeze in. At times I'd set three or four traps fairly close together.

I'd collect moss and dry dirt under a windblown tree, made sure it was dry, pulverize it, and keep it in cornmeal sacks. I'd cover my traps with Kleenex and sprinkle this mixture over the trap. Usually the trap worked all winter. Wind would blow snow off of it off and on, and eventually it would appear natural.

I threw bait some distance, maybe fifty feet, from the trap or traps. They'd sniff the bait, and maybe get a whiff of my scent, but a wolf wouldn't be suspicious of the natural-looking trap set.

Another set that worked well was where I poured a bucket of sour moose blood, collected in the fall when I killed a moose. I'd pick a gravelly spot on a ridge, dig a hole, and pour the blood into that, and set traps there. Wolves could smell it, and they'd spend some time scratching and pawing to get at that nice smell – and stick their foot into one of my traps.

Sometimes a wolf in a trap will wag his tail when you near, but more often I found they struggle. Occasionally they'll pull hard enough to get out of a trap, and run off. After I had trapped for a few years, and had a few wolves pull out of my traps as I neared, I got so I'd stop about a hundred yards from a trapped wolf, and lie down and use a hard-point bullet to finish him. It didn't hurt the skin, and it put an end to wolves pulling free and running off.

Wolves are extremely difficult to stalk. Their eyes are as good as those of a man, and their sense of smell is beyond anything we can imagine. There's nothing wrong with their ears, either. And they seem always to be alert. While I've killed quite a few with a rifle, it was always when I surprised a wolf or wolves.

I was once sitting and watching a bear on the Alaska Peninsula, when a wolf came trotting along a bear trail. It didn't know I was anywhere near. I killed it with one shot at about 100 yards.

Years ago when there wasn't much going on, I used to do a bit of wolf den hunting in spring. The bounty was as good for a pup as for an adult wolf, and twenty dollars was a lot of money.

Wolves usually dig their own dens, although, for their use, they'll occasionally modify a fox den, or even an old bear den. They prefer a place where the brush is thick, on a south-facing hillside where there is good drainage. They won't dig a den in gravel; it has to be silt. They'll dig back in and the hole is almost big enough for a small man to crawl in. One of the dens I dug out went twelve feet back. There are usually bones scattered near the entrance of a wolf den.

Once, when two of us dug three pups out of a den, we weren't able to get the adults. However, as we left, the adults, howling mournfully, followed at a distance, howling. Admittedly, it made me feel a little sad. Wolves love their pups, and take very good care of them.

"You walk on and carry the pups," I told my partner. "I don't believe they're very good at math."

We had come to an open meadow. He continued to walk, while I hid in the brush. The female, following him at a distance, trotted within 150 feet of me and I killed her with a rifle. Four bounties —eighty dollars. That was good money in the 1930s.

7

The Parbuckled Brownie, and other Bear Oddities

I GUIDED PHIL JOHNSON, a Fairbanks banker, on a 1953 spring hunt on the Alaska Peninsula. He and I chased a huge old bear all one day. It was during the bears' rutting season, and I guess that big old boar was looking for a sow. (The bear is the only big game animal in Alaska that breeds in the spring.) This big bear had twice as many feet as we did, and he stepped a little longer, so we never did catch him. We put in a long hard day chasing. Next day we decided to rest in camp.

While we sat around a campfire talking, I looked across the little lake we were camped near, and saw a big brown bear. He had worked his way down a hill, and was busily feeding on various greens. We left the campfire and managed to sneak to within fifty feet of him.

Phil had some hand-loaded ammunition, but he may have slopped a little beer in it while doing the loading. The first shell he tried mis-fired. The bear heard the firing pin hit, raised his head, looked around, and went back to feeding. The next shell he tried was kind of a hang-fire; there was a noticeable pause after he pulled the trigger until the rifle fired.

The bullet hit the bear all right, but it was a glancing shot that broke a shoulder. The bear ran.

Phil shot nine times at that bear. Some of the hits were flesh wounds, and one bullet hit his ribs, but there wasn't a vital shot in the bunch.

Slim and a client with a large brown bear, probably on the Alaska Peninsula. The big guide enjoyed hunting brown and grizzly bears, "... because they have a little fight back, and they think for themselves." He said, "A bear has poor eyesight, but a super nose and good ears." ROSEMARIE OLSEN

The bear started across a little swamp. I didn't help matters any when I yelled, "Hold your fire." I wanted him to wait until the bear was on dry ground; I didn't want to skin that bear in the swamp.

When the bear reached dry ground, I yelled, "Shoot, shoot. Hurry, shoot!"

The bear was walking on a bear trail on top of a little ridge when Phil finally made a solid it. It would probably have been lethal. But brown bears are tough, and it usually takes several hits in vital areas to stop one.

This bear reared up, and rolled off the ridge into the lake we were camped on. He started to swim across, but he was like an old tire with a lot of leaks. Bubbles came out of bullet holes all over him. I hollered at Phil to finish him, and he finally shot him through the hump and the bear collapsed and floated.

I returned to camp for a rope, and cut the longest willow pole

I could find (there are no trees on the Alaska Peninsula). I waded to the bear, tied the rope through his mouth, and put a few half hitches over his nose, and started wading. Water was up to my waist. Ice had been gone from the lake for only four of five days. That water was cold.

As I waded, Phil pushed the bear off the bank with the willow pole. We floated it a good quarter mile and beached him at camp. I got more ropes and ran two of them under him while he was floating, and we parbuckled him like you would roll a log right into camp.

My next move was to get into dry clothing and stand next to a blazing fire to thaw my lower half.

That bear's hide squared almost ten feet, and Phil had a full-size mount made from it to put in his bank.

Phil's shooting was pretty wild, both on the record ram he and John Brennan bagged in 1950, and on that big bear. While skinning the bear, I discovered the bear's penis bone had been shot into two pieces.

"You didn't kill that bear. He was so upset after where you hit him that he decided to commit suicide; he tried to drown himself," I told Phil.

It's unusual when a hunter kills a brownie with one shot. Even when shot in the heart, a bear may run or walk hundreds of feet before dropping, or it may even charge.

To illustrate, a couple of my hunting clients and guide Warren (Tillie) Tilman and I, had an unusual experience on an Alaska Peninsula hunt for brown bears. One of the hunters, with his teenage son, and I had hardly walked out of camp one day when we saw a big brown bear feeding toward us. We sat and watched him until he was within seventy-five yards. He then hit a trail and started moving off. The hunter shot, and the bear collapsed, looking to be about as dead as any bear could be. It lay perfectly still.

Tillie was in a boat with the other hunter on a nearby lake. They could see us, and heard the shot, and we saw them start our way. They had the only cameras in camp, so we decided to wait for them and the cameras so we could get pictures before we started skinning.

After five or ten minutes the bear moved one front foot. Soon he kicked his hind feet. Then he rolled over, and remained still for a time. In a few minutes, he got to his feet. He swayed, and fell.

We watched, surprised, thinking the bear wasn't capable of going anywhere. We were still waiting for the cameras.

Shortly, the bear again got to his feet, and staggered into a little patch of brush. Still, I didn't tell the hunter to shoot again. We moved to a little knoll where we could see the bear better. After a bit, he came out of the brush and started down the trail, walking about as fast as a man could.

Tillie and the other hunter had landed and were walking toward us; it appeared they were going to meet the walking bear. When they saw what was happening, they stepped aside, and my hunter shot the bear, and this time finished it.

His first shot had hit the bear in the small of the back, and slightly to one side. We concluded the bullet had shocked the spine and temporarily disabled the bear's nervous system. It was probably half an hour between the shot that paralyzed the bear, and the one that finished it.

That bear's hide squared eleven feet.

While hunting brown bears in the spring on the Alaska Peninsula I learned early to look for places where bears have slid down steep snow patches. It seems to be courtship behavior.

While on this hunt, Tillie and I watched a big dark boar repeatedly slide down a long steep slope. It was quite a ways off, and we watched through spotting scopes. A light colored female stood at the top of the hill watching as a much bigger and darker boar twice slid on his fanny down a long slope as she stood and watched. Each time, he walked back to her. It sure looked like he was a show-off, and she was admiring him.

I've never seen this behavior in the fall. Of course, there isn't much snow during fall bear season on the Peninsula.

I once watched with amusement as a big boar made his slide at the head of Little Mother Goose Lake. There is a long steep draw there, and as the bear skidded around a bend, he came to a ledge of rocks sticking out of the snow. He put on the brakes with all four feet, throwing loose snow all directions, and stopped a few feet short of the rocks. He walked across the rocks, and sat to slide the remainder of the way down the slope.

I figured that maybe he had slid over the rocks at some time, and knew the feel of them.

Unused snow slides are usually dirty, with leaves, dust, dirt, and what-all on them. A bear skidding down a snow slide uncovers fresh, clean snow, which is glaringly obvious, even from a great distance.

A bear has poor eyesight, but a super nose and good ears. If there are berries he'll likely be in a berry patch, but if there are salmon in a stream or lake, that's where he'll be. Brownies follow valleys a lot, where they dig wild peavine. They'll also dig and eat willow roots that are no bigger around than a man's thumb, and up to maybe six feet long.

When hunting a brownie, I try to get as high a vantage point as I can, where I can see lots of territory. From there I do lots of glassing, and don't run all over the country and scatter my scent and that of my hunter. I've found that a brownie will move out quicker from man's scent than almost anything else. A man's scent may not drive a trophy bear out of the country, but it can make a night feeder out of him; most big bears are night feeders anyway.

In the fall, however, when he's trying to lay on fat, as long as he isn't disturbed by man scent, or someone stomping around his territory, he'll feed in the daytime. For that reason I try to never go around where a bear is likely to move around and feed.

A big brown bear will have a home canyon. He'll use it as a base, and maybe work out of it for food, but he'll always return. That canyon may be as rough as goat country, but it's his. He'll put the run on any other bear that shows up. Either that, or a bigger bear will put the run on him and take the canyon over.

You can kill a big brownie in his home canyon, and return in a couple of years and find another big brownie living there. There might not be another big brownie for ten miles or so, until you come to another suitable canyon.

I had a party on the Alaska Peninsula hunting brown bears in 1953. We were high on a ridge when we saw a big bear rapidly walking down a distant ridge. As we watched, we saw a smaller bear ahead of the big guy. The little bear ran a ways, stopped, and stood on his hind feet to look back at the big bear. The old bear never did run; he just took a long walk, following. The little guy repeatedly ran and stopped to peer back. He never let the big guy catch up with him. That performance took place over a good two miles—a big bear putting the run on a smaller, younger bear.

We were too distant to shoot the old bear; he was a real buster.

Sometimes bears behave oddly. In 1951 I had a hunter at Crescent Lake in the Aleutian Range on the west side of Cook Inlet. We spotted a trophy size bear some distance up a stream. We followed the river, walking on sand and gravel bars. Suddenly, an old sow with two yearling cubs appeared on an eight-foot-high bank across the river.

She ran to the edge of the bank and, standing on hind legs, snarled angrily. She batted at willows, and stomped about, telling us that we were no good so-and-sos, and we'd better stay away from her and her cubs.

The cubs ran back and forth behind her. Once they stood as she did, on hind legs, one on each side of the angry old lady.

We were about forty feet from her, against willows on the opposite bank. She slapped one of the cubs and it ran off a ways. She ran back into the brush and was gone perhaps thirty seconds, but returned to continue her aggressive act.

The cubs seemed inquisitive. Every time they came out to look at us she batted them and they ran back into the brush.

We stopped walking and stood, rifles ready, hoping she wouldn't cross the river to get to us. The river was shallow on our side. Beneath the bluff where she stood it was about six feet deep. If she jumped into the river she'd have been in deep water, and we'd at least have had a chance to shoot before she reached us.

I didn't want to shoot her, and wouldn't unless she charged. Also, we had in mind the trophy bear upriver. If we were forced to shoot the sow, it would alert the bear we were after.

The old girl finally let us by. She stayed back in the brush, although she kept blowing and snorting as we went on.

As we neared the trophy, I saw him trying to catch salmon. Unlike other bears I've seen fishing for salmon, he was trying to put his foot on a fish. Every other bear I've seen catching salmon grabbed them with their jaws. And here was one using his feet.

Not only that, it looked as if his tongue was hanging out. As we got closer we saw him set his foot on a fish, or, perhaps he caught it between his feet. He picked the salmon up with his jaws, holding his head high and eating it like a seagull would, chewing and shaking his head.

"That bear must be crazy. I've never seen a bear eat fish like that," I told the hunter.

When we were close I instructed the hunter, "When he gets out of the creek, on either side, shoot."

He had a .375 Magnum, so there shouldn't have been any difficulty in killing the bear.

At his shot the bear went down, but he got up and rolled into the creek and was swept into a bunch of driftwood. He swam, and starting to climb the steep opposite bank.

"I'll go over and see if I can get him to charge me. When he gets out of the water, shoot him. Don't let him chase me too far," I told the hunter.

I crossed a riffle on the creek, intending to try to tempt the bear into chasing me across an open bar. Instead, it turned and splashed out of the creek nearest the hunter, who then dropped him.

When we looked him over we saw what his trouble had been. Someone had shot the front part of his lower jaw off, behind the tusks; both tusks and all the front bottom teeth were hung on his lip, and pointed forward. We could see where he had dragged them in the gravel.

It must have happened in late fall, and he went into hibernation and it healed that way. I don't know how he could have survived otherwise. Even so, it was unusual for him to survive. Surprisingly, he was in good condition. Obviously he had been able to get enough to eat.

The old brownie is one tough critter.

In the early 1950s, I took a hunter on a brown bear hunt to McNeil River, on the west side of lower Cook Inlet. Dozens of bears were feeding on dog salmon (chum salmon) along that river. Hunting was easy—we simply picked the two largest bears we could find. (the bag limit then was two).

After that hunt I suggested to the Alaska Game Commission that it set McNeil River aside, to be used as a bear viewing area, and that it be closed to bear hunting. The commissioners agreed to this, and in 1955 the McNeil River drainage was closed to bear hunting.

[AUTHOR: McNeil River is still closed to bear hunting, and is world-famous as a brown bear viewing area, thanks to the foresight of Slim Moore.]

I hired John P. as cook and general helper for the McNeil River hunt. Early on the hunt the hunter killed a small moose, mostly for meat. We dressed it nicely, and kept it covered in a pup tent.

John P. accompanied the hunter and me one day as we sought a big bear. We turned down half a dozen animals as being too small. On the trail home, John P. walked rapidly ahead so he could get a start on cooking supper. The hunter and I took our time, walking leisurely and enjoying the late afternoon walk beside the beautiful river.

A small brown bear had torn the end out the pup tent, crawled in, and yanked out a piece of moose meat and was working on it when John P. arrived in camp. The bear charged, and John P. started shooting.

I've never heard a bolt action rifle work so fast. John P. fired nine shots, and there didn't seem to be a break in the shooting to reload.

"There must be another hunting party here. No one man could shoot nine shots from a bolt action rifle that fast," I told the hunter.

The hunter and I arrived in camp to find a dead brownie lying next to a drift log. It was full of bullet holes. A still-shaking John P., holding an empty rifle, anxiously told us all about his close call with the bear.

Our camp, on the beach, was near a pile of drift logs, left by high tide. They covered about an acre, and in places they were ten or twelve feet deep, all jackstrawed among each other – a real tangle.

This was a wonderful chance for me to have some fun. I acted as if I was angry as hell, and I really chewed on John P.

"You weren't supposed to do any shooting on this hunt. You also knew we were only a few hundred yards behind you. For what little time it would have taken us to walk here, until we reached camp you could have outrun that bear in the drift pile. That way the hunter could have shot it."

If there had been an airplane handy, I think John P. would have quit me then and there.

He sputtered, not sure what to think. We might not have had a meal that night if I hadn't relented. The hunter and I laughed. John P. somehow couldn't see the humor.

I've seen both interior grizzlies and coastal brown bears walk near a salmon river all loose-jointed, as if they were going to fall apart the next step. When close to the stream I've seen them kick into high gear and run hard to leap into a foot or two of water that held a bunch of salmon.

Salmon boil in all directions. The bear tries to grab one, and sometimes succeeds, for bears are mighty quick. Other times, they seem to have planned their next move. If there is a shallow riffle near, they may run there to catch salmon they have spooked away the hole they had just bombed.

On one of my Alaska Peninsula bear hunts, my hunter and I were walking up a stream when I saw a bear run from the far side of the creek and leap into a big hole. He churned the water to a froth, reaching for salmon, but he didn't catch any.

He soon emerged from the hole on our side of the creek and ran down a trail straight toward the hunter and me. I knew he was heading for a nearby riffle, hoping to catch salmon he had spooked from the hole. The hunter, of course, didn't know that.

I wasn't anxious to have that bear close to my hunter; one never knows what a bear will do. I ran toward the bear as hard as I could, with the bear still running toward us. The bear and I got within about fifty feet of each other. I threw my hands up and hollered. The bear, apparently astonished, stopped and stood on hind legs and snarled.

A rock about the size of a football was directly under the bear, and I put a bullet into it. Splinters from it may have stung the bear.

The bear leaped, made a complete turn, and ran full-out back down the trail and crossed the creek. It looked as if he knocked most of the water out of the hole where he crossed.

My client, eyes big, caught up with me. "What do you know about that bear wanting to charge me that way. He must have been crazy!" I said.

The hunter looking a little dazed, blurted, "I don't think the bear was crazy!"

That hunter believes to this day that I charged a charging bear. He told everyone we met after the hunt, "Slim is the craziest man I've ever seen; a bear charged us full speed. Instead of shooting or running, he charged the bear!"

You can never tell what a bear will do. You think you've got 'em figured out, and the next one is altogether different. Here's a good example:

Fred Hollander and I were on the Kenai Peninsula, walking over a ridge and breaking down into Funny River. We saw a little grizzly bear digging for a parka (ground) squirrel. About all we could see was the bear's hairy rump.

"You want to see something funny?" I asked Hollander.

Without waiting for his reply, I let out a yell and beat on my leg with my hat. I thought I'd startle the bear and watch it carry the mail over the nearest hill. The south end of a running bear is kind of funny; the hind legs look as if they're on a wheel when a bear really sprints.

That bear flew out of the hole like it was snapped out with a rubber band. It reared, looked at us, peeled its lips back, and started to smack them.

"What do you know? That little son-of-a-gun wants to fight," I said, surprised.

I took a few steps toward the bear, and made a little more noise. The bear ran sideways, stood on its hind legs, and snarled. It zig-zagged toward us and semi-charged several times, each time stopping a bit closer. We let it get within about 100 feet. It was uphill from us, and I became uneasy.

That little bear finally charged and stopped at about fifty feet—too close for comfort. It appeared ready for a genuine charge, so I shot it. It was a young sow with a hide that squared about seven feet. There was no sign it had ever had a cub. We were surprised at its behavior; most bears hightail it when surprised the way I surprised that one.

"What in hell was funny about that?" Hollander asked.

8

Close Encounters with Interior Grizzlies

ONE FALL, A FELLOW LIVING IN AN OLD TELEGRAPH STATION at Paxson, ten miles down the then gravel-surfaced Richardson Highway from my Summit Lake lodge, accidentally walked up on a little grizzly feeding on moose bones and scraps he had thrown out near the station. The bear reared up, snarled, and charged him.

The man was fleet of foot, and beat the bear to the door. He remained inside until the bear left. Word of this soon reached me and others at Summit Lake.

A day or so later, a truck driver, stopping at my lodge, told me, "I just saw a sow and cub grizzly a few miles down the road. They seemed kind of headed your way, but when they saw my truck, they headed for the hills."

Dan Luddington, who occasionally worked for me, and lived with his wife nearby, had moose meat hanging in a screened cache at my lodge. The nearby presence of the bears worried Dan; he feared they would come to Summit Lake and raid his meat cache.

There wasn't any danger of that. My lodge is an out-of-the-way place for bears, and they don't normally come near. Dan's reaction was kind of a hold-over from the old days when bush residents figured that a dead grizzly was a good grizzly. The bears were dangerous to men and horses, they occasionally tore up a camp, or even a cabin, and they especially liked fresh hanging meat.

So Dan took his semi-automatic .351 rifle, caught a ride on

Slim (right) and a client, with a large interior grizzly. ROSEMARIE OLSEN

the highway, and picked up fresh sow and cub grizzly bear tracks where the truck driver had seen the animals leave the highway. They were probably not the same bear or bears the guy down the highway had seen. It had been snowing, and was still lightly snowing. Dan followed the tracks for between half and three-quarters of a mile, and came to a little draw where there was a dense curtain of head-high willows. The tracks went into the willows, and he followed them—a serious mistake on friend Dan's part.

He went along peering at the fresh tracks, parting the brush with his hands. The tracks soon ran out at the old bear. Dan was within twelve feet of her when she reared up and reached for him. He didn't see the cub.

He raised his rifle and pulled the trigger.

"My gun mis-fired," he told me.

A binocular hung by a strap from his neck. "When the bear hit me, it knocked them across country," he said.

I don't think they were ever found. He had marks across his chest where the bear made that swipe.

The bear knocked him down and started chewing on his head, the usual place a grizzly works on a human victim. She was a small bear and couldn't get her jaws open enough to take in Dan's entire head.

However, she cut his scalp to ribbons, and she must have hung a tusk in Dan's eye socket because he got a blood clot in the back of his eye which caused the eventual loss of that eye. One of his ears was badly torn, and his left arm was severely chewed from wrist to shoulder.

While the bear chewed and mauled, Dan stubbornly clung to his rifle.

"I finally doubled up, got my feet in the bear's belly, and kicked her off of me," he told me.

The bear grabbed a foot and started to drag him. By then Dan had his rifle working. He fired a shot into the bear's chest, killing her.

He was badly hurt and desperately needed help. He knew he was close to the highway, actually much nearer than the route he had followed in trailing the bear. But he was bleeding so badly he feared to try a short cut. He figured if he followed his back track he couldn't get lost. If he didn't make it, he, or his body, could be found on the trail he had left. So, he staggered along his back trail to the highway. It was a long, torturous hike.

The moment he reached the highway, a truck came along heading for Fairbanks. The driver picked him up and took him to Big Delta. On the way, he managed to stop a truck heading south and arranged for the driver to stop here at Summit Lake to tell his wife what had happened.

He was given a blood transfusion at Big Delta, and flown to Fairbanks, where he remained in the hospital for a few days. He was then flown to Swedish Hospital, Seattle, where he mostly recovered.

He didn't want his wife to see him while he was in such bad shape. When he returned home he couldn't convince his wife there wasn't a bear behind every bush. They lived one more year at Summit Lake, and left for good.

When I learned of the mauling, I went to see where it took place. I was amazed at what I found. I've never seen a place so torn up. About forty square feet looked as though two bull moose had been fighting. Parts of the site looked as if Dan and the bear had fought over them two or three times. Moss, grass, and willows were broken down, pulled up, and flattened. Bark was skinned off of the willows, and a many were torn from the ground.

I found the bear carcass. Bennie Benson, who worked on the highway, skinned it the day of the mauling. Signs indicated that the cub had been eating on it. Its tiny tracks had flattened the snow and beaten the ground down all around the body. I also saw its track half a mile away.

That's raw nature—a cub having to eat its mother's body to survive.

If I, or Bennie, had seen the cub, we'd have shot it. It was that spring's cub, too young to survive without its mother. Others who went to the site later told me the cub ate the entire carcass.

IN ANOTHER GRIZZLY MAULING I'm familiar with, Earl Hearst [still living in Fairbanks in 1956] was attacked before I arrived in this part of the country (1926). He described the event for me when I lived in Fairbanks.

Hearst established the first trading post at the Native village of Chistochina years before I arrived in Alaska. More recently, he and two other men were prospecting along the Chistochina River (in the Alaska Range). Each was leading a packhorse, as they traveled single-file down a trail. Earl and his horse were in the middle. A sow grizzly ran out of the brush behind the last fellow in line, and ran past him toward Earl.

The fellow behind him yelled and Earl turned only to have the bear knock him down, and start chewing on him. And, like the bear that attacked Dan Luddington, it chewed on his head. Earl wore his red hair pretty long, and it gave the bear something to get her teeth into. She pulled off a big piece of his scalp.

The bear and Earl rolled around so fast and furiously the others were afraid to shoot for fear of hitting Earl. They hollered and screamed. The bear dropped Earl and started for the others. One yanked his .30-30 off his packboard while Earl and the bear rolled about. He killed the bear before it could maul anyone else.

The other two guys hurried to get Earl to medical help. Before leaving the scene of the mauling, they grabbed his scalp, stuck it on his head, and tied a towel to hold it there. They had a long way to go, with no roads, and, of course, no communications. It took about a week for them to get to Chitina, from where Earl rode the railroad [which no longer exists] to Cordova.

A doctor removed the towel, and his torn-off portion of scalp came with it. There was caribou moss and other debris under it. Also, the doctor said, it was on backwards.

It hadn't re-seeded.

To this day (1956) Earl has a bald place on top of his head; the rest of his hair still grows around it, as thick as ever.

EVERY YEAR DOCTOR GILLESPIE, who practiced medicine in Fairbanks, made a little bear hunt with me. First, however, we'd talk hunting, and discuss where we might go. We might play a few hands of cards, or take short walks from my cabin. Maybe we'd fish a bit. Doc was on vacation and needed to relax. Finally, we'd decide where to go on our bear hunt of the year.

A cheerful Slim Moore wearing rain pants. He remembered being on hunts on which he didn't get dry for a month. ROSEMARIE OLSEN

One year, about ten miles from my Summit Lake cabin, we found where a big bear had fished for late spawning salmon in the Gakona River. It had gone up a hill to sleep, leaving fresh tracks in a foot of new snow. We quietly followed the tracks to some thick brush.

"We're about to rouse that bear, Doc," I whispered.

He had been kicking about the deep snow, and didn't take me seriously; he thought I was trying to encourage him.

The bear made a lot of noise when he got up out of sight in head-high brush, about twenty feet in front of us. He snorted, and ran uphill. Still out of sight, he knocked snow off the brush as he ran. At about eighty yards he was about to pass a small opening.

"Get ready, Doc. I'm going to shoot alongside of him as close as I can without hitting him. I think I can put him into that opening," I called.

"Ok," says Doc.

At my shot, as I had hoped, the bear jumped smack into the middle of that opening. Doc promptly shot him in the fanny, giving him a flesh wound. It didn't stop him, but it did make him angry.

Old griz turned around about as quickly as any bear I've ever seen, and charged straight for us. He was out of sight in one jump. He knocked snow from the brush as he plunged downhill toward us. The falling snow told us where he was, but we couldn't tell how far he was under the brush.

I jumped on a stump, and, followed the bear's progress with my rifle. He was awfully close, and I had yet to get a glimpse of him. Suddenly, about forty feet away, his big head loomed in an opening. I didn't squeeze that shot; I almost jerked the trigger off.

The bear stopped. I couldn't see, or hear it. It simply disappeared.

Doc and I stood there a bit, wondering. Shortly I suggested, "Let's back out of here and get up on that knoll. We'll have a little better fighting chance there."

Nothing happened while we moved. On the knoll above where I had last seen the bear, we waited, listening and looking. Nothing.

"Keep me covered while I go down to see what happened," I told Doc, and, with my rifle's safety off and ready for use, I slowly slipped through the brush to where that big head had disappeared.

The bear was lying dead by a windfall he had started to jump over when I fired. My bullet had hit the corner of his mouth, knocked a couple of teeth out, and continued back to break his neck.

A head shot, or anywhere up and down his back, is the best shot to stop a charging bear. A shot in a grizzly's hump will break him down and let you put in a lethal shot.

That bear was so close, and moving so fast, that I was ready to pull the trigger on anything I saw through my .30-06's peep sight. Fortunately, it was his head.

I suggested to Doc that he have just the rear end of that bear mounted, "That's where you hit him," I kidded. We were good friends or I wouldn't have gotten away with that crack.

~

Another interior grizzly made my life interesting for a few moments. I was guiding a Texan named Holmes in the Alaska

Range when we saw the bear walking up a ridge about 250 yards away. Holmes' shot knocked the bear down, but it rolled into a draw and ran down hill into a patch of brush.

We eased up to the brush patch, and I saw a little patch of fur. I heard the bear growling. Holmes remained back while I moved closer, rifle ready. When I was about fifty feet from it, I saw the bear lying flat on its back, its feet waving in the air.

"Do you want me to finish it?" I called.

"No. I want to do it," he answered.

He came in behind me and tried to locate the bear with his rifle scope, but all he could see was a blur of brush.

The bear, still growling, started to roll side to side.

"That bear's going to make his feet," I warned. "You'd better shoot."

Holmes kept trying, but finally said, "I can't see it in my scope. You'll have to shoot it. Use this hardpoint so you don't ruin the skull."

He handed me a cartridge.

As I started to pull my rifle bolt back to insert the hardpoint, the bear got to its feet and streaked through the brush toward us. Holmes put me in mind of a Fatty Arbuckle movie. I swear he leaped into the air and made three or four steps before his running feet hit the ground.

I dropped the hardpoint on the ground, slammed the bolt of my rifle shut on the original cartridge, saw the bear's approaching head in my peep sight, and yanked the trigger, all in less time than it takes to tell it.

The bear slid to a stop about fifteen feet away, my 180-grain factory load in its brain. It wasn't a big bear, but it was big enough.

"Where did you figure on going?" I asked Holmes, straight-faced.

"I was getting out of your way so you could shoot," he answered, very seriously.

I didn't blame him in the least for his hasty departure; it was a logical and wise move under the circumstances.

9

The Midnight Charge of a Brown Bear

THERE WAS A TIME WHEN I'd rather hunt Alaska's coastal brown bears than anything else. Bears are individuals, and you never know what a bear will do. No two act alike. Sometimes they have some fight-back in them, which can be a real challenge to a hunter. Also, I think a bear thinks a little for himself.

Sometimes when you shoot one he'll fall, be completely limber, and roll and tumble down a hill. He'll look as though you made a killing shot. You think he's down for good. Commonly, it seems when he wants to make his feet, he can do so at any time. Then he might get on his feet and charge, or get into the brush before you can get in another shot.

As I age, I'm no longer sure of my choice of the brown bear as my number one. The big problem is, you have to bring the hide out in one piece. The skin of a big brownie that squares ten feet or so always weighs more than 100 pounds. Hides and meat from other animals you might cut in two, but that darned brown bear hide has to come out in one piece. I could handle those big hides when I was younger; it isn't so easy now.

I always leave the fat on the carcass, which cuts down on a hide's weight. I broke myself years ago of cutting the fat off and taking it back to camp on the hide. I sharpen my skinning knife on a bevel, and keep the beveled-side up, which makes it easier to skin close.

Dead bears don't always fall in a dry spot. A lot of time they'll get in a mud hole, and it'll be raining. When it's like that, and a big brownie's hide becomes saturated with water, it can weigh between 150 and 175 pounds. When you're packing such a load, it doesn't help that the footing is always mean on the Alaska Peninsula, where I've done most of my brown bear hunting.

I once had an interesting brown bear hunt on the Alaska Peninsula with a client, Newton Harral, of Claude, Texas and his teenage son. This great thrusting 400-mile peninsula, which ends in the long string of Aleutian Islands (the world's longest archipelago), lies between the cold Bering Sea and the warm North Pacific. It's a stormy world as a result of the sea temperature variance, and deep low pressure areas commonly form there and blow east to follow the peninsula toward mainland Alaska. This brings rain, roaring winds, snow, and misery to hunters, pilots of small planes, and coastal commercial fishermen.

This spectacular, mostly un-peopled peninsula, with its handful of small coastal Native villages, is a land of untroubled civil peace. Except at its base, near the mainland, there are no trees. Dense alder stands fill valleys and hillsides. The Aleutian mountain range forms its central spine. Large and small streams pour both north and south from these mountains, which run to 3,000 feet or so, with an occasional volcano thrusting to 7,000 feet.

Early on that spring hunt I tried to find a bear for Harral's son on his fifteenth birthday. As we hunted that day from our fly-in tent camp, with father and son trailing close behind me, we saw two bears in the distance on a big snowdrift. We had to cross a valley to get to them. I've never seen wind blow any harder than it did as we crossed that valley. It must have been whooping at sixty-miles-an-hour. As gust after gust slammed into us, we staggered to keep our feet. Talking was nearly impossible.

The two bears moved, and we continued over a little knoll. Suddenly, they were within about fifty yards. It was a boar and a sow. The sow, on the left, was the largest.

"Shoot the one on the left," I told the boy.

I had already briefed him on where to hold for a lethal shot. I didn't know how well he shot, but I was soon to find out.

He was eager, but nervous. The wind was still howling, and

when he jacked a load into the barrel and lifted his rifle to shoot I saw it waving in the wind like the nearby alders. My heart sank. He fired. The wind and his excitement conspired against him; his bullet hit a rock under the sow's belly.

I should have made him lie prone for that shot.

I've never seen a bear move faster than that big sow. She must have taken some shrapnel in her belly. She jumped about ten feet and, at the same time, made a half turn and ran down the snowdrift. Both the father and son then shot at it, but between their excitement and the high wind, both missed.

The father then missed a shot at the boar, as it ran over a ridge. In a few minutes I saw him run around a mound below us. He was leaning on his side, with his side almost touching the ground. It put me in mind of a man on a leaning motorcycle rounding a drome. He looked jet-propelled.

Two bears and eight missed shots. The hunters blamed the wind.

A brownie can move fast, but I never saw any move faster than those two. I've timed a running grizzly on a highway for a short distance with my pickup at thirty to thirty-five miles an hour. Bears can also run steadily for a long distance. It seems to me when a bear is really pouring it on—a black bear more so than a brown or grizzly—when he gets at his best speed his hind feet almost look as though they are on a wheel making a full revolution with every jump. It has a comical appearance when viewed from behind.

Later on that hunt, we were in high country inland twenty miles from the Bering Sea coastal village of Ugashik. It was one of the two or three really hot days that occasionally occur on the Alaska Peninsula during hunting season. Through our glasses we watched a distant bear feeding on skunk cabbage near a large stream. He fed a little, then ran and jumped into the stream. It looked as if he'd knock all the water out of it. He looked to be a nice big bear—a real trophy. He'd feed for a time, then again leap into the river to cool off.

It was about four o'clock, and the bear was at least three miles distant. We headed toward him, walking swiftly. However, it was one of those times when the bear managed to stay out of range. He kept working uphill and we climbed after him. Repeatedly, we'd get to where he had been, and see him a little farther along, just close enough to make us think we might catch up.

By about 7 o'clock we were finally within about 350 yards of him. We were tired from the long day's walk, and the climbing didn't help. The bear was digging a hole in a snowdrift.

"Do you think you can hit him from here?" I asked the hunter, hopefully.

"I don't think my rifle will shoot that far," he said.

He had a scope-sighted .300 Magnum. "Don't worry; the rifle will carry that distance ok," I told him. "Hold a bit over him," I advised.

He fired two shots. Both bullets hit the snowdrift near the bear. The bear looked where the bullets hit, but didn't react. I don't think he even heard the shots. The high wind likely carried the sound away.

Fortuitously, the bear started toward us. "Hold your fire," I told the hunter. The bear soon went out of sight, and we waited. In about five minutes he topped a ridge, still walking toward us.

The hunter wanted to shoot then, but I wouldn't let him. "Let him come closer," I said.

The bear went out of sight a couple more times, but continued walking toward us. When he was within seventy-five yards the hunter and his son started shooting. I don't believe they hit him because he didn't change his gait as he went into a little draw that was almost at our feet.

Finally, one of them shot him down through the hump, a killing shot. My mood turned black when we reached that giant bear. He had dropped about four feet into a hole in a snow bank. His hind feet stuck in the air, and his head was between his hind legs.

How was I to skin him in that half-buried, contorted position? It didn't help that I was tired from a long day of hunting. A guide's life is not all roses.

I managed, but it was one of the most difficult skinning jobs I've ever had. That bear's hide squared ten and a half feet (average of greatest length and width). He was truly a huge brownie.

It was all I could do to get to my feet with the hide rolled and tied to my Trapper Nelson packboard; it weighed at least 150 pounds.

We started for camp following down a valley where a little stream ran. Within a couple miles where the stream was sufficiently deep to float a rubber raft, I cached the hide, planning to return for it next day with the raft I had in camp.

We then followed down an ancient, worn almost knee-deep, brown bear trail. It was like a well-beaten packhorse trail. The wind was at our back, and I didn't worry about bumping into another bear. Near midnight, five moose came out of a side trail, and ran ahead of us on the bear trail. I figured they had winded us. We could barely see them in the darkness, but they made a lot of noise as they clattered off.

We traveled single file. I led, the teenager followed, and his father was last. We were at the foot of a hill, near a noisy little creek that poured into the river we were following.

"Look, look, bear!" the youngster shouted.

The kid's yell may have saved our lives, or at the least, a savage mauling. The sound of the creek had masked the noise of the bear's charge, and it was pure luck the kid saw it. That bear was probably chasing the five moose, or at least it was aware of them. I believe he mistook us for the moose. He could have been upon us within seconds. Brown bears are swift and savage in an attack; they can knock a man's head off with one swat of a powerful snowshoe-size front paw.

It was so dark I barely saw the bear leaping toward us. He was within thirty yards, and was pouring it on as hard as he could. We were in head-high brush, which he was smashing through like a bulldozer. I jerked my rifle off the packboard and laid one in his direction. I couldn't see the sights; I simply pointed. In the darkness, it seemed as if fire spurted a good six feet from the gun's muzzle.

The bear stopped, stood on hind legs, and growled. He probably heard the shot and saw the fiery muzzle blast. I pointed against black and touched her off again. That time he bawled loudly and stuck his head between his hind legs. We heard him rolling over and over the in the crackling brush.

We couldn't see him, although he was within thirty yards—a mere five or six jumps from us. He growled and roared loudly while rolling. I threw a couple more shots into the general area as he thrashed about.

"Run backward with your rifles ready," I yelled at the hunter and his son.

We had just crossed an open meadow. I thought we'd have a better chance to fight him in the open. When the hunter and his son were a couple of hundred feet back, I followed, running backward on the rough tundra and shoving shells into my rifle.

I couldn't do that in daylight on level ground.

The three of us stood in the meadow, facing the bear, rifles ready. He continued to roll about, bawling and growling. Those fierce sounds raised hackles on my neck. We heard him, now on his feet, as he crashed through brush almost to the trail where we had been when we first saw him. From there he turned and ran up the little noisy creek bottom. He didn't run around brush; he went over it, still growling as he ran.

"How come you didn't help me?" I asked the hunter when we could no longer hear the bear.

"I was scared. I guess I didn't pull my bolt far enough back to put a shell in the barrel, and it snapped empty," he ruefully explained.

It was still a long way to camp. We stood and talked it over. All three of us were badly shaken. I suggested we go on. "I'll hang my handkerchief here so we'll be able to find this place come daylight," I said.

"Before you hang that handkerchief up, you'd better let me wipe my leg with it," he said. He sounded serious.

"We'll just split the handkerchief two ways for that," I said.

I hung my handkerchief on a big alder, and we went on. The youngster wanted to stop and build a fire. He was a swell kid. I had never heard him swear or complain about anything. Finally he said, "God damn. I've never seen so many bears in my life. There's one under every bush!"

I agreed with him.

We went a little way, came to some dead willows, and decided to make a fire and wait for it to get lighter. I was so tired it didn't make any difference to me. I lay down and went to sleep. As long as he didn't have to move outside the firelight to gather wood, the kid kept the fire going.

We walked into camp at five in the morning. A plane came for the hunter and his son that day and they left.

Two other guides and a client went with me when I packed the rubber raft in to float the bear hide out. Near my handkerchief I found the big bear's tracks where he had charged through the brush toward us. There was very little blood where I knocked him down. So much dung was scattered in the brush where he'd been that you wouldn't think one bear could hold that much.

The four of us tracked him as far as we could, but bear tracks were everywhere, and we eventually lost the trail. Blood spots ended before we lost his trail. From his tracks he was possibly a nine-footer [hide size] judged by the size of the pad of the hind foot.

Bear size on Kodiak Island and the Alaska Peninsula can crudely be judged by the size of the pad of the hind foot. For every inch of pad, not including toes, a bear carries about a foot of hide (average of length and width). Elsewhere, as on Montague and Hinchinbrook Islands for example, where brownies commonly walk on mud flats, their feet are like snowshoes; a small bear might have absolutely huge feet. The inch of pad vs. foot of hide rule doesn't hold there. The Montague Island brown bears are the scrawniest bears in Alaska. I don't believe there's a nine foot bear on that island.

The first time I hunted there I picked up a big, fresh, brown bear track on the beach, and followed it. When I caught up with the bear I couldn't believe what I was seeing; "That can't be the bear that's making those tracks," I told myself.

To grow big bears, an area has to have a lot of feed. If there are poor salmon runs for a few years, the bears seem to come smaller. I think the reason Kodiak and Alaska Peninsula bears are so big is the abundance of salmon in the streams in both areas. The brownies in both areas also come out of hibernation early in the spring, and go into hibernation late in the fall. I've had trappers tell me that some Kodiak brownies are still out of their dens in December.

Hide size doesn't count for Boone and Crockett trophy status.

Skull size is the sole criteria. Hunters not interested in a Boone and Crockett listing are generally eager to get a huge bear skin, and there are various ways to make a bear hide longer while it is green. Dr. Will Chase, of Cordova, who did a lot of bear hunting, once killed a whopper of a bear, the hide of which I saw where it was stretched on the side of the Alaska Hotel in Cordova. The front legs and head end were nailed high on the wall, and a pole fastened to the hind legs and rear end of the skin. A couple of pry poles against the bottom pole stretched the hide lengthwise.

It stretched fourteen feet, but it was only seven or eight feet wide.

I've seen skins cut half way up the belly so that belly flap falls out behind to make a longer skin. To make a bear hide square, it should be cut on the back side of the hind feet and come about three inches inside of the vent, so the end of the cut should be about the end of the tail. There are many ways to kill a cat besides choking him on butter.

When properly skinned, the front legs should lay out and come about even with the nose. When a skin is removed wrong, the front legs may lie at a ninety degree angle (point straight out), or even angle toward the rear, which is a funny looking trophy that makes the bear appear to be swimming.

I always make the skinning cut for the front legs where the long and short hairs meet. That way his arms (front legs) come out about even with his nose. The skin is also a little wider that way.

Trophy bear skins are usually tanned and backed with velvet or some other cloth, and used as a rug, or sometimes hung on a wall.

The hide of a brown or grizzly bear is usually wider than long. Black bear and polar bear hides are the opposite—they're longer than they are wide.

I don't think there has ever been a brown bear with a skin you could throw out on a floor, pull the wrinkles out, and square fourteen feet. It takes a huge bear to square eleven feet. You're generally spreading a fresh bear hide on a gravel bar, and it's usually raining. One thing is sure; by the time a bear skin is tanned and made into a rug, with felt backing and all, it's usually considerably smaller than the stories told about it.

10
One-shot Bill, a Trophy Bull, and the Ways of Moose

My client for a thirty-day mixed-bag hunt in 1948 was Bill Young, a slim and friendly Californian in his sixties. He drove a four-wheel-drive Dodge carryall 4,580 miles from the California-Mexico border, to my cabin at Summit Lake. It was piled high with what he thought he might need on our hunt—extra clothing, pots and pans, a Coleman stove, a couple tents with poles, a sleeping bag, and, of all things, a saddle. He had three rifles, two of which were semi-autos; the third was a .300 Magnum bolt rifle, with a Lo-swing Pachmayr all-weather Alaska scope. He arrived happy and excited, wearing Levis, high-heeled riding boots, and a Stetson cowboy hat.

He was a pleasant hunting companion. I found him a big-antlered, white-necked caribou, a thirteen-year-old Dall ram whose golden horns made a full curl (a sheep's age can be determined by annual rings on its horns), and two grizzlies (the bag limit), both with hides that squared more than eight feet. He neatly bagged each, proving to be a fine shot, in fact, we nicknamed him One-shot Bill. I think he'd have gone hungry before he would have killed an animal that wasn't a good trophy. And, unusual for the time, he wanted to be sure that every piece of meat was brought right in and taken care of. He was a fine sportsman

Now we were looking for a trophy bull moose.

I then owned a weasel, a World War II military surplus tracked rig that could go almost anywhere. Its wide tracks and light weight

89 One-shot Bill, a Trophy Bull, and the Ways of Moose

"One-shot Bill" Young's prize bull moose spread 65 inches, with numerous tines. Though not a photo of Young's bull, the bull in this photo was probably about the same size, and obviously, it has many long antler tines. James Faro

didn't tear up the country, either; it was difficult to find its tracks across the tundra four of five days after it had passed. I preferred to hunt with horses, but good horses were hard to find by the late 1940s and into the 1950s, so I had started using the weasel from my Summit Lake Lodge, which, at the time, consisted of a two-room cabin. The weasel took us into good game country and I always parked it and hunted afoot.

Keeping up with the times, in later years I chartered airplanes to take me and my clients on hunts, and I set up my hunting tent camps on various lakes where a float plane could land.

Young did ok for his age, but half a day of hard hiking was about his limit. We looked over a lot of moose, but for about a week I found nothing outstanding.

I've killed, or my clients have killed, about 150 moose, and

I learn something about moose every time I hunt them. Before moose rutting time, the big old bulls like to be close to a little pothole lake where they can feed, and near a patch of brush for his beds. A bull will go to the lake and feed, after which he will return to his favorite bed area for much of the day.

Often a bull will use the same pothole lake and brushy area for beds each fall for four or five years, and he may remain within an area of not over 150 yards. He may have dozens of beds that he'll use regularly. Green timber areas are favored, which makes the old bulls hard to find just before the rut.

Before the rut, then, I try to watch pothole lakes, where there is good moose feed, and where a big old bull may be moving a short distance from the lake to his beds.

With Young, I checked a lot of areas where I expected to find an old bull, without seeing a single decent trophy. We saw many small bulls, for they are the first to get on the prowl for the rut; they start chasing around while the old bulls are still charging their batteries.

About ten days before the rut the big old bulls hardly move, but lie around building energy. They're especially hard to hunt at this time, which is from about September 8 or 10 to about the 16th.

Four days before the end of moose season (September 20), I drove the weasel from Paxson east about twelve miles where we set up a camp near Wolverine Mountain, preparing to hunt the Gakona River country.

Tall spruces surrounded the camp, there was plenty of dry spruce handy for fires, and a clear spring with icy water flowed a few feet from our tents. A cow moose and two calves fed nearby.

Later that day, with the weasel we crossed small streams and circled little lakes. We splashed through shallows of the Gakona River, which arises in the Gakona Glacier, high in the Alaska Range. Typical of glacier streams that pour from these mountains, it is braided, with many gravel bars.

Moose sign was everywhere, and game trails spiderwebbed the valley, some of which were more than a foot deep in the moss and grass.

By then, we had looked over about dozen ordinary bulls. Only a few days of moose season were left. "Any bull would suit me now," Bill commented. We were getting a little desperate.

On the evening of the 16th, we sat in a little meadow, using binoculars to study the country across the Gakona River. "There's a bull and a cow at the foot of that hill," I said. When guiding, it encourages clients when I point to game, even if it isn't trophy quality. Most hunters enjoy seeing a variety of wildlife.

This was an ordinary bull, with antlers that spread about forty-eight inches. He was a mile or more distant. About then, to my surprise, near that little bull a string of five cows trotted single-file down the hill.

"What would cause a string of cows to be on the loose at this time of year?" I wondered aloud. About then, I saw the huge antlers of a big bull behind the cows. He was driving them toward the flats. That answered my question.

He was the trophy I had been seeking for Bill. The cows were his harem.

When he stood sideways to us and turned his head, his antlers came almost over his short ribs (the back part of the ribs). That's a big rack. Moose antlers appear smaller head on than from any other angle; and they appear larger when a bull is going straight away.

When the big bull saw the little bull, he trotted toward him, and soon ran all out. The little guy ran like hell, and the boss bull chased him down the river bar for a quarter of a mile. The old bull then returned to his cows. Now he had six.

The big boy attacked a stand of willows. It looked as if he tore half of them out by their roots. He picked them up with his antlers, and tossed them over his back and every which way.

"He's laying down the law. There won't be any walking out on him. He's showing those cows what could happen to them," I told the hunter. I guess he believed me, for he didn't ask questions. I've never seen a bull punish a cow, but maybe they do.

As we watched, that huge bull milled about, herding his cows, and moving constantly. He didn't feed. Unfortunately, he was too far for us to try for him that day. Near dark, we watched him drive his harem single-file up the hill and out of sight. As they climbed, the great palms of his antlers flashed a ghostly white in the fading light.

Bill and I were up early next morning. Rain slanted down, and at times it was half snow; after a bit, snow started sticking to the brush.

I took the weasel several miles upstream in the Gakona valley to near where we had seen the big bull, parked, and we walked. We couldn't glass very much; every time we pulled binoculars out they filled with wet snow. We found a lot of fresh moose sign, and walked in slushy snow. Soon, there wasn't a dry thread on either of us, and it was damned cold.

Had the big bull and his cows left for distant places during the night?

We were near timberline, and there were patches of green timber in the area—the kind of places where bulls like to take their harems. We checked three of these timber patches, quietly sneaking and peering. In two hours we were nearly frozen, and we returned to the weasel.

By this time the snow had thickened. Visibility was two hundred yards or less. I thought about returning to camp and a nice warm wood stove-heated tent. We had seen nothing to encourage us. We thawed in the shelter and warmth of the weasel's cab. Hot coffee from a thermos helped.

We hadn't checked one little stand of green timber. "Let's walk to the head of that little patch. We can slip up to it and give it a good look. If we don't see that bull we'll have to give him up for the day. Maybe the weather will break tomorrow," I suggested.

We walked quietly through falling snow for about half an hour, and stopped where brush grew among some scattered spruce trees.

"If I were a bull moose with a harem I'd sure take it into a place like this. Let's wait here for a minute," I quietly told Bill.

To better see, I climbed a nearby mound, wiped my glasses dry, and carefully looked all through the timber and brush. At first I was disappointed. Then I saw, poking slightly above the brush, what appeared to be the branches of a downed tree. I held my glasses on it for a few moments, and thought I saw it move. I held my breath to steady the glasses, and saw the "branches" move again.

I was looking at the antler tines of the big bull. He was bedded about 100 yards from us, his body and antler palms concealed by brush. All that showed were the tips of his polished tines.

Moose ears are big for a reason; they are the most sensitive ears of any of Alaska's big game. Several times, while sitting at the edge of a quarter-mile-wide lake watching a moose on the far side, I've deliberately broken a little stick. The moose's head would fly up right now, with those huge ears focused my way. Of course sound crosses water more readily than through brush and trees, but it's a good illustration.

I was surprised the big bull hadn't heard us and slipped away. The falling snow probably silenced our movements.

I motioned to Bill to join me and, in whispers, described where the bull was bedded. For a time he couldn't see those antler tips. I almost had to draw him a picture. He finally saw them, but I couldn't convince him they belonged to a moose.

"That's an uprooted tree," he whispered.

"I'll tell you what. You stay right here, and if that uprooted tree gets up and starts to leave, you cut it down," I instructed.

Having seen how well he had shot on the other trophies I had found for him, I was confident he could easily drop the bull.

I left him sitting on a log, rifle across his lap. Snow continued to fall, at times so heavily the hundred-yard-distant antler tips were impossible to see. I slowly worked my way to the side of and within about fifty yards of the bull. When he got my wind or heard me and spooked, I expected him to go toward the hunter.

The cows started to stand here and there. Then the bull got to his feet. When he started to shoot, the lenses on Bill's rifle scope were blocked by snow and he couldn't see through it. He had to push the hinged scope to the side, and use his iron sights. That took but a moment. The bull had just made his feet when Bill fired, breaking his neck with a 180-grain bullet.

That huge bull dropped in his tracks as if he had fallen through a trap door. The sound of the shot resounded among the nearby hills, the first break in the silence of the day. It was three days before the end of the moose season.

At Bill's shot, seven cows (the bull had picked up another

during the night) boiled out of the brush. Most ran toward Bill, and several passed within ten feet of him, giving him a thrill; a thousand-pound cow moose noisily crashing through brush toward you in full flight is impressive.

When they got over their fright, most of them stood around, probably wondering what had become of their boyfriend.

The heavily-built and beautifully symmetrical antlers of that bull spread sixty-five inches, with numerous tines. It was as nice a moose rack as I've ever seen, and the best I've ever found for a client. We measured seven feet even (with a tape) from the tip of his front hoofs to the top of his hump. Standing, he would probably have stood six feet eight or so. You'd have to have a good big horse to stand that tall at the withers.

We estimated his weight at close to 1,800 pounds. I sent a hind quarter (two ribs and the quarter, just as you would butcher a beef) of that moose to Fairbanks cold storage about a week after we killed it, and was billed for 220 pounds. Front quarters weigh more. I believe that moose dressed more than 1,000 pounds. A common rule-of-thumb on moose weights says that the dressed weight of a bull moose equals about half its live weight.

Despite Bill's one-shot kill, I don't recommend shooting a bull moose in the neck during the rut; his neck is normally swollen then, and a bullet may not penetrate the tough expanded muscles to reach bone and nerves for a killing shot. An old bull I once killed while in rut took three shots in the his swollen neck—each of which knocked him down—but he continued to leap up and run until a fourth bullet finally penetrated his neck to smash some of the vertebrae to drop him for good.

When a moose starts on the rut, his neck starts to swell, and about the time he associates with cows, his liver turns from dark red or brown, to almost a gray or milk color. It becomes so soft it is almost impossible to take out in one piece; your fingers will go right through it.

If a moose has a gray liver, we figure the meat will be strong. Sometimes his neck will be swollen, but the liver is ok—then the meat is fine.

One-shot Bill's bull had a solid liver, and his meat was fine.

The surest shot for a moose is in the deepest part of the animal. This can hit the heart (low on the chest) or the lungs (higher). A lung-shot bull may stand around for a short time, or walk a short distance, before dropping. But a bullet can easily penetrate the deepest part of a moose, and a lethal shot there is almost guaranteed. It is definitely the most certain.

Bill was about as tickled as any client I've ever guided. We forgot all about being wet and cold, and ignored the falling snow while we caped, dressed, and quartered that big bull. He was so heavy I had to use the weasel and a chain to turn him over while skinning and quartering.

Bill couldn't haul all the meat of that moose back to Texas in his carryall—it would have spoiled before he got there. We gave most of it to St. Joseph's Hospital in Fairbanks, and to a few old-timers who I knew needed meat. I later shipped a hundred pounds of it by air to his home in Texas.

TODAY (1956), MOOSE ARE FOUND in parts of Alaska where they have never been known to range before. They are now found farther north and farther west than anyone can remember. Old-timers around Naknek, at the base of the Alaska Peninsula, where moose are now common, don't remember moose in that area in the past. And their range has expanded far beyond Naknek, for they are now found all the way west on the Peninsula to Port Moller.

Also, within the last few years moose have moved north of the Arctic Brooks Range. They are now found on the north slope among willows along the Colville River and other streams. It must be tough going for them, for they are scrawny, noticeably smaller than moose elsewhere in Alaska.

Is Alaska becoming warmer?

[AUTHOR: I remind readers that the stories in this volume were current as of December, 1956. Sharp observers like Slim Moore started wondering about the warming of Alaska half a century ago. Now, in the 21st century, there is no doubt that Alaska's climate has warmed. Hints of the change were becoming evident in the 1950s.]

I've heard a lot of arguments about how much a big moose weighs on the hoof. Using a spring scale, nationally known hunter/naturalist Fred Hollander and I once weighed a Kenai Peninsula trophy-size bull. After killing it, we skinned head and cape, and cut the carcass into pieces we could weigh.

It was in mid-rut, and the stomach was empty. With an estimated seventy-five pounds for blood and other fluids, which we had no way of weighing, that bull weighed 1,680 pounds on the hoof.

Babiche (rawhide, used for snowshoes, for lashing dog sleds together, and hundreds of other uses) made from moose hide is among the best. To make it, pick the hair along the center of the back of a moose where the skin is the thickest. Hair must be picked while it is still loose, moments after the moose dies. From that piece of hairless skin, cut strips one half or three-quarters of an inch wide. First soak the babiche in water, then nail one end from a ridgepole or high branch of a tree, and hang a 100-pound block of wood from it. It will stretch and become just as round as a rod. Let it dry that way.

To use it, wet it a bit, and pull it into a snowshoe frame, or wrap parts of a dog sled with it—or whatever. As it dries it shrinks and will almost bust a snowshoe frame.

Bull moose can be called during the rut, and there are several ways to do it. Indians I know use a dry stick or a shoulder blade and rattle them together or thrash them on trees or bushes. It is effective in one way, for it can sound like a bull polishing his antlers, or even a little skirmish between bulls.

But, in another way, a moose that has just taken a licking in a fight, hearing rattling antlers close, may run. Little mulligan bulls get chased away by the big trophy bulls all the time, although they will hang around the outskirts of a harem if they can, especially as they get a little older.

Most of the time even a bull that has suffered a beating will come to a call, but once in a while they skedaddle.

You can bring in a bull moose almost any time during the rut by chopping wood, but most of the time it's not a trophy. While chopping wood at a camp I had on the Kenai Peninsula, I once brought a small bull in so close I grabbed a rifle, thinking he might attack me. He apparently suddenly got my scent and fled. I didn't think I smelled that bad.

To call moose, some hunters like to grunt like a bull. At the peak of the rut, older bulls grunt constantly, whether or not they are with cows. When a bull grunts, other bulls may answer. Each bull figures the other might have a cow.

The cow bawl is not easy to imitate, but if one can do so, it's the most effective way of all to call a bull.

An acquaintance, Harry Revell, once told me how effective his birch bark moose call was, and offered to show me.

"It's too early in the rut," I told him.

"You don't know my call," he said.

"Ok, I'll go with you," I agreed.

We went to the east side of Jarvis Creek (north side of the Alaska Range) where there are some big hay meadows and little pothole lakes.

He let out a few blasts. An old cow and her calf were feeding nearby. They lifted their heads, listened for a moment, and ran like hell.

"You need to tune 'er up a bit, Harry," I kidded.

About then we heard sticks breaking on the far side of the hay meadow we were on. The hay had just been cut.

"See, I told you," Harry bragged.

I began to believe maybe he did have a bull coming. "Try again," I urged.

He gave another blast. As we watched, from the far side of the meadow two Swedes appeared, hauling hay in a cart pulled by a yoke of oxen.

I never let him forget the time he called two Swedes and an ox team out of the brush.

Most big old trophy bulls hunters kill almost always have broken ribs from fighting other bulls. They may be freshly broken, or healed from past seasons. Sometime or other another bull slammed into him. Because of this, don't think you're going to bring an old trophy bull on the dead run to you with a little bit of a call. Bulls have had a little experience with their cohorts. When coming to a call, a bull circles downwind, and he'll try to keep under cover as much as he can. He wants to keep track of the "moose" doing the calling, thinking maybe he can slip in and cave in a rib on the caller.

Sometimes in calling a moose, when I get a grunt in answer, I'll make a quick sneak downwind and wait. I've had wildlife photographers with me who I stationed downwind when I called. That's normally where an approaching bull shows up. He's usually sneaking, and testing the wind.

You can be a little too ambitious with a call; if you call too often a bull can get suspicious and you'll probably never see him.

If a bull isn't too wise I can generally get him to come in. A lot of times I'll grunt and they'll walk a few feet and stand and grunt; they kind of cough it out. They'll cough and listen. If a cow hears that cough, if she's not a member of a harem she'll answer. Once in a while I've seen an old cow on a long trot throw her head back and let out an awful bawl, kind of like a jackass. Another cow moose call is for the calf.

I've known Indians who could run a bull moose crazy by making kind of a squeak by running their thumb nail across the side of a dried moose shoulder blade; it about runs a bull nuts. It is a kind of saw-ey noise, deader than a scratched blackboard. I've never heard a cow or a bull make a noise like that.

BLACK BEARS ARE HARD on newborn moose calves. Grizzlies are hard on them in some places, too. But generally the big bears remain higher on the mountains than cow moose.

The Kenai Peninsula is great black bear country. During the

Slim preparing to skin a black bear killed by client Walter Holmes. He sharpened the blade of his skinning knife on one side so the edge was beveled, allowing him to skin close, leaving fat on the carcass instead of the hide. SLIM MOORE

1920s fox farmers there fed their foxes a lot of black bear, without seeming to cut bear numbers down.

In the spring of 1941 Andy Simons, a top notch guide, and a long time member of the Alaska Game Commission, with Game Warden Hosea Sarber, went to the Kenai Peninsula during moose calving season. They found black bears hunting moose calves cooperatively; two bears working like bird dogs, noses working, as they searched for calves. The two men killed twenty-eight of them. Twenty-two of these bears had moose calf parts in their stomachs.

In the mid-1930s I hunted on the Kenai Peninsula quite a bit, and I saw seven or eight black bears in sight at one time.

THE MOOSE IS PRETTY CAPABLE of taking care of himself, although bulls lose a lot of caution during the rut. Most other times, when he's not feeding, he's lying down. And those big ears aren't hung on him for nothing.

Especially in winter with snow on the ground, it is next to impossible to get near a moose, except perhaps along the road where they're used to noise. A bedded or standing moose can hear you snowshoeing a lot farther than you can hear him get up and move away from you.

Snow telegraphs snowshoe noise. Often, when I know where a moose is hanging out, I might go for days and never go near the place until a wind comes up that rattles the brush enough to kill snowshoe noise.

Moose are amazing animals. As big as they are, you'd think they'd stand out in brushy areas, or timber. Often they blend with the scenery. They can sneak out through brush, and never crack a twig. Yet, when he knows he has been seen, and is trying to get away, a fleeing moose can make as much noise as a tractor as he plows through the brush. Somehow, a bull with antlers that spread five feet or more can slip through dense timber without banging against the trees, or catching in the brush.

ONE CAN TELL THE AGE of a moose until he's five; after that it's guess work. A year-old moose has two large front teeth in the center (lower only—moose have no upper front teeth). A two-year-old has four; a three-year-old has six. A four-year-old has eight. Ten teeth at five years is a full mouth.

TROPHY BULL ANTLERS are at their largest and best probably when a bull is from seven through ten years old. I think antler size depends somewhat on climate conditions. When there is a hard winter, with deep snow, moose can be in poor shape by spring. It seems to me there are fewer really big antlers on the bulls during the fall after such winters

With a mild winter and light snow, and an early breakup, we seem to find more good moose heads in the fall.

A U-SHAPED NECK is a constant characteristic of a cow moose; it doesn't vary with age. By this characteristic, you can identify an old antlerless bull in winter, or distinguish a bull from a cow of the same size. Same with caribou. The cows have a lighter neck, with a pronounced U on the upper side. Bulls' necks run straighter from the shoulder hump to the ears than that of cows. The reason is obvious; cows don't have to hold up fifty pounds or more of antlers in the fall.

WHEN I FIRST LIVED in the Summit Lake and Paxson area in the late 1920s and early 30s, there were very few moose. In winter, when I found a fresh moose track in the snow, if I needed meat, I'd trail him. At times I'd stay on a trail for several days, siwashing it near a fire without blankets wherever dark caught me. More times than I like to remember, when I caught up with them, moose managed to sneak out on me, and I wouldn't get a shot.

This bothered me. I started paying more attention to moose behavior, and eventually stumbled on the reason they were able to sneak off.

While working my trapline one winter day I came across fresh moose tracks in new snow. I hadn't seen a moose track for months, and I needed meat. I drove my dog team home, and returned on snowshoes to follow those tracks.

The moose, browsing on willows, had wandered back and forth in a valley. I followed the tracks for several miles where he stayed mostly along a river bottom, among the thickest willows. I jumped and raised my rifle when half a dozen willow ptarmigan flushed near, their white wings flashing and black tails contrasting with the snowy land.

A friendly head-swiveling hawk owl perched atop a small spruce as he watched me pass. On silent wings he flew ahead to land on another small spruce, apparently simply to watch me pass.

There is plenty of life around to keep a man interested during the short days of winter. Besides these birds, there are snowshoe rabbits, northern jays (camp robbers), croaking and bell-ringing ravens, and an occasional eagle on high.

Finally, the moose's tracks turned sharply to the right, and he worked up a rise through scattered spruces. I stayed on his tracks, which made a several hundred yard half circle. Soon his tracks were some distance from the trail he had left in the valley, and he had walked in reverse direction.

I found his bed. His tracks from the bed indicated he had left in a hurry.

That son-of-a-gun, when he had fed enough and was ready to bed down, had stopped feeding, climbed, made a half circle, and picked a bed where he could watch his back trail. He was in his bed when he had obviously seen me on his trail. He was long gone, of course, when I reached his bed.

Perhaps such behavior is a defense against wolves, about the only animal other than man that might normally follow a moose's trail. I gave up on that moose, for I wasn't prepared for a long chase that day. I went home, still meat hungry, wondering if this was unusual behavior.

It wasn't.

A couple of months later, I trailed another moose in fresh snow. When it stopped feeding and the tracks abruptly turned right, I turned left, and made a huge circle. I sneaked back to where I guessed he may have bedded down. He heard me coming—snow transmits the sound of snowshoes—but I was within shooting range when he got up, and I had my winter's meat.

Because a moose stops feeding and turns right (or left; some moose may be left-handed!) doesn't mean he's planning to bed down; he might keep going. But if he stops feeding, and moves in a half circle, chances are good he's looking for a bed where he can watch for any critter that might follow him.

If he hasn't bedded down and you have circled, you can always pick up his tracks again to continue following him.

After that, when I trailed a moose in winter my success rate was considerably higher.

And some hunters think moose are stupid.

11
The Johnson-Brennan Record Ram

IN THE FALL OF 1950, a nonresident hunter who planned to hunt sheep with me cancelled due to illness. My camp was already set up. I had bought grub, hired Winn Barr to cook, and arranged for Art Smith and his float-equipped airplane to do the flying. I decided to proceed with the hunt, and arranged to take resident hunters instead of the nonresidents I usually guided. Two of these were Phil Johnson, a Fairbanks banker, and John Brennan, owner of a Fairbanks clothing store.

My camp, in the Alaska Range's Johnson River drainage, was on a rather mean 1,800-feet-long lake at 2,200 feet. It lies on a little bench under a ridge, and at times a down-draft falling off the ridge pinned our float plane to the lake. On days without that draft, once off the water, the plane was in business, for the terrain drops steeply; with nose down, it could quickly gain good flying speed and be on its way.

In earlier years I had hunted there with horses, and I knew it had produced big rams. It hadn't been hunted for some years. The 1949 sheep season had been closed Territory-wide, and to my knowledge no one had hunted sheep there for a couple of years before that.

Art Smith flew Johnson and Brennan to my lakeshore camp about noon August 20, opening day of sheep season. From camp we saw feeding sheep on a distant ridge. They were on the far side of what we called Boiling Creek, a little river that is pretty rough to cross. The name is appropriate, except it isn't hot.

"Those are rams," I told Johnson and Brennan. The white sheep were fairly far apart, and there were only three or four of them, thus I knew they were older rams. You never see a really big bunch of truly big, old rams; they generally run in groups of two to five or six, rarely nine or ten, and there may be as much as 100 yards between them as they feed.

Ewes and lambs feed in a close bunch. If you're near enough you can see lambs right on the tails of the ewes. Even small rams feed close together.

Since Boiling Creek was hard to cross, and we didn't want to start out wet in the morning, we decided to cross the creek that afternoon, and make a spike camp at the foot of the ridge below the sheep. That would give us a head start in the morning.

After the struggle to cross the creek—jumping from rock to rock, and some wading—we found a nice camp site, with a nearby clear-water spring I had previously used.

In mountains, most of the time wind or cold air blows downstream, so the wind was in our favor, and we were within a mile or mile and a half of where we had last seen the feeding sheep.

The ridge we climbed next morning was steep. Johnson and Brennan were both soft. The more they sweated, the more they hollered about how hard it was to climb that ridge. I kept prodding them.

Three rams were in sight when we reached the top; two were feeding, and the other, lying a bit higher, was the lookout. They were about 200 yards distant, across a little valley. There was no chance of getting closer. We'd lose ground if we went into the valley, plus, we'd have been in plain sight.

"Lie down and take good rests. You should have no trouble hitting them from here. You have plenty of time," I suggested.

I put my glasses on the lookout and I couldn't pull them off. My eyes ran out like those of a snail. I'd never seen such perfect sheep horns. He was by far the biggest of the three. He was facing me, so I had a clear view of him.

"Be sure to get the one that's lying down. He has an outstanding head," I pointed out.

Head mount of the famed Johnson-Brennan record ram. It was taken in the Alaska Range's Johnson River drainage in 1950. It is the only trophy listed by the Boone and Crockett Records of North American Big Game that is attributed to two hunters. WILLIAM BACON III

The hunters started to argue about who was to take the first shot. After a couple of minutes of this, I was about ready to shoot both of them.

They moved out of sight and flipped a coin to determine who got first shot at the big ram. Johnson won. He threw himself prone and took a long time aiming. His bullet exploded on a rock behind the sheep; I don't know if he put padding under his rifle barrel, or if it was on bare rock; anyway, he overshot.

In one swift move, the big sheep leaped to his feet and jumped straight ahead. Brennan fired at him, but his bullet hit in front of the ram. That turned the sheep, and started him back the other way.

Confusion reigned. Both hunters repeatedly shot at the big ram. Every time he started to go away, someone overshot and the sound of the bullet hitting a rock chased him back toward us.

The three rams bunched, and one of the smaller rams, with about a three-quarters curl (legal in 1950), was hit in the mid-section.

Five or six shots were fired. One of the hunters finally put a bullet into the chest of the big ram and it dropped dead. Both were shooting so nearly at the same time it was hard to know who had killed it.

"Someone finish that other sheep. It's hit through the mid-section. Don't shoot it there again," I called.

Brennan kneeled behind a rock and shot it through the head, finishing the job.

It was clear from the time it was killed that the big ram would rank high in the Boone and Crockett Records of North American Big Game. Under the old system, where length of horns and maximum spread were the criteria, it would possibly have been the number one Dall ram. But under the newer system, in 1950 it was the third best Dall ram head ever listed, scoring 180 ⅜ points. [Author: Today (2005 Boone and Crockett records) it is ranked twenty-one.]

Dried, the right horn measured 45 ⅞ inches; the left horn 46 ⅞. Circumference of the right base was 13 ⅛; the left base 13 ⅝. Greatest spread 29 ⅛.

Being a relatively young thin-horn ram, it did a lot of shrinking. U.S. Fish and Wildlife Agent Ray Woolford and I measured it before and after the mandatory sixty-day drying period. In that time, the diameter of each of the horn bases shrank a full inch.

We didn't give ourselves any of the best of it because it leaned against a radiator in a Fairbanks bank for those two months; it did all the shrinking possible.

Johnson and Brennan, being friends, decided to claim the head in both of their names. When this request went to the Boone and Crockett club, they said the problem had never come up. They accepted the record in both names, and it is the only listing in the book with two hunters credited for one animal.

WALTER HOLMES, a hunter-client I had from Texas, killed a very

Walter Holmes, and a fine ram taken in 1937 near Morningstar Creek in the Jarvis Creek drainage, Alaska Range. Rosemarie Olsen

big Dall ram while hunting with me in earlier years. It would have out-scored the Johnson-Brennan head, except that one horn was broomed. It measured 46 inches on one side, and 41 on the broomed side. Base diameters were 14 ¾ inches

It was an August, 1937 hunt, and we'd just had a heavy snowfall. Sheep were fast moving down the mountains out of the snow, and it looked like they'd get out before we could find a trophy.

In the Jarvis Creek area, we came upon nine rams lying on a little ridge near Morningstar Creek. The biggest was closest to us. As we watched, he chewed his cud, and fell asleep, allowing his chin to gradually drop into the snow. His head then flew back up like it was on a spring, and he went back to chewing his cud. He repeated this several times.

We lay behind a rock until we began to shiver. I was afraid my client wouldn't be able to shoot if we waited any longer. One of the sheep, off a bit by himself, had nice forty-inch-curl horns. At the time, a hunter was allowed to take two rams.

I told Holmes, "We know what that one is (the forty-inch one). He's out by himself so we can see him good. There are some awful nice looking rams in the bunch. Why don't you shoot the big one that's close, and when the others get up, we'll pick another —probably that one off by himself."

He shot the closest ram, and it didn't even move. Its head dropped was all. When the other eight stood, the one by himself looked like a moose in a caribou herd.

"There's your sheep," I told him.

He shot it, and it jumped into a canyon. It didn't appear to be hit. I ran the 150 yards to where he had disappeared and saw it still rolling end over end about 300 yards into the canyon.

The one that rolled into the canyon had a perfect forty-inch (length of curl) head, and other had a forty-six inch and a broomed forty-one inch horn. In two shots Holmes had killed two top-notch Dall rams, which is kind of a record in itself.

Holmes had the big head mounted, and hung it in his Texas office. He got tired of people asking him where he had acquired "that nice goat head." They apparently thought it was some kind of domestic goat. That burned him up, and he pulled it out of his office and hung it in his home.

It may be a hill-billy idea, but I think broomed or broken-tipped horns found commonly on big rams may be because that horn gets in the way of their vision. I've noticed that a wide,

Slim Moore, with his first Dall ram, he killled in 1927 at the head of Castner Glacier, Alaska Range. ROSEMARIE OLSEN

sweeping horn is seldom broomed. Rams with a tight curl that comes close to the eyes are most often the broomed ones.

※

YOU HAVE TO BE CAREFUL when eyeballing a group of rams when trying to pick a trophy. Fred Hollender and I once made a mistake in judging a ram. We had come upon eleven rams—an unusual number to be together—lying on a little knoll. There was barely room for all the sheep there.

We studied them with glasses for a long time, and decided that one was really outstanding. It had one horn to us, and we could see it clearly. Another sheep was bedded close by and behind it. It appeared that the outstanding ram had two huge horns—we thought we could see both.

Hollander said he could kill the ram easily without touching the one behind it. When he shot, the ram he killed rolled over; what we had thought was his other horn ran off on another ram.

The horn on the side we had a seen measured forty-five inches. The horn on the far side, which we couldn't see, was broomed off about half way.

※

NOW, BACK TO THE 1950 HUNT At the head of Johnson River. Art Smith flew Phil Johnson, John Brennan, and their sheep out; then flew another couple of resident hunters to our camp, one of whom was Fairbanks Doctor Paul Haggland.

A few days later, the two hunters and I, with cook/packer Winn Barr, were off on a two-day hunt. Art was alone in camp. He flew to Delta for supplies, and came back late in the afternoon. We had a sheep hanging in camp, and a little grizzly bear had torn it down and was chewing on it. The bear had also been through camp, biting almost everything he could find, like milk cans, which had squirted milk all over everything.

Art landed and slid the plane's pontoons up into the grass. The little grizzly was in an umbrella tent, and so was Art's rifle. The bear came out of the tent and walked to meet the plane. I guess he'd never seen one up close.

Art sat in the plane and revved the engine. The bear cocked his head this way and that, peering at the noisy thing, and took a step or two toward it. Finally, the noise was too much, and he walked into the brush.

Art straightened camp and re-hung what was left of the sheep. At dark he went to bed, but noises in the nearby cooking outfit soon awakened him. He got up and, in bright moonlight, saw the bear walking between him and the cook stove. He stuck his rifle out the tent door and fired. He missed the bear, and shot a hole in the stove pipe.

The bear ran off, and Art went back to sleep.

The sound of sticks breaking behind the tent again woke him. He got up and peered out the window, from which the bear had earlier torn the screen.

His nose almost touched that of the bear, which was standing on hind legs peering in.

The bear ran. Art dived out of the tent and threw lead. He hit the bear, but it kept going into thick brush. Art didn't dare follow.

"If there had been two of us, with flashlights, I might have tried to follow it. I wasn't about to try it alone, in the dark," he told me.

Art crawled back into bed, but he got little sleep. The bear lay in the thick brush groaning and grumbling for most of the rest of the night. At daylight, rifle ready, Art sneaked into the brush and found the bear, dead.

He spent kind of a rough night.

We had one other bear encounter on that 1950 sheep hunt. Doc Haggland and another hunter killed two rams some distance from camp one afternoon. I caped them, and we packed both horns, and the meat of one ram, back to camp.

Next day, Art Smith, Winn Barr, and I returned to pack in the second ram. It was a long hard trip to where the rams had fallen. We had seen no bear sign, and foolishly went to retrieve the meat without taking a rifle.

At the gut pile and the skinned head we had left of one of the rams, we could tell from tracks that a little bear had eaten from them. Bear tracks hardly bigger than my hand led up to the ridge toward where we had left the other ram.

I had draped the second sheep carcass over a rock on the other side of that ridge, about fifty feet below a kind of rim. We climbed the ridge, and, sure enough, the grizzly was lying crossways on top of the sheep. We were about seventy-five feet from, and fifty feet above, the bear.

It was a small grizzly. We yelled at it, and it stood on its hind legs and snarled, saying, "That's my sheep."

Since it was a small bear, we decided to chase it away with a few rocks, get our sheep, and return to camp.

We walked back up the ridge and gathered armfuls of rocks, returned, stood on the rim, and peppered the bear.

Instead of running away, he climbed toward us. It was pretty steep, and we thought for a time we could stop him, and we poured the rocks on. They bounced off of him, but didn't stop him. When he got within about fifty feet, we decided it was time to leave. He stood on his hind legs and snarled, but didn't come any farther.

We had no choice. We had to let him have the sheep until we could get a rifle. He had won.

We retreated. First, we had a mean glacier to cross. It didn't seem to have any ice, but there were rocks that weighed three or four tons, and every one of them seemed to be balanced; they teetered when we stepped on them. We jumped and tippy-toed across the glacier and its crazy rocks, and went a mile or so to a nice meadow where Winn Barr and I waited while Art Smith returned to camp to get his plane.

He arrived in five or six hours and dropped our sleeping bags (the delay meant an overnight stay away from camp for Winn and me). My rifle was rolled in my sleeping bag, but Art had neglected to tie a splint on it. My sleeping bag swapped ends several times in the air and hit lengthways. My rifle stock broke at the trigger guard.

I cut several straight pieces of willow, and with packboard lashing rope splinted the gun together.

Back across the glacier we went. The bear had eaten the gut

pile, but hadn't chewed any more on the sheep. He was asleep on top of the carcass.

We hollered, and since he had run us off once, he figured he could do it again. Growling and acting fierce, he came toward the rim where we stood. I shot him, and he rolled a ways and dropped out of sight over a cliff. We heard him hitting here and there as he dropped.

Suddenly, rocks rattled, and seven big rams broke over the top and into sight. The bear must have dropped directly among them. Undoubtedly they were surprised; to say we were surprised is putting it mildly.

So, we had most of a slightly-bear-chewed sheep carcass, plus a small bear hide to pack back to camp.

The 1950 hunt from my Johnson River sheep camp was one to remember.

Woes of a Guide

ABOUT 1946, I GUIDED A BUSINESSMAN who told me he had started at the bottom and worked his way to the top. He was very efficient. He drove from the states up the new Alaska Highway to my cabin on the Richardson Highway.

The day he arrived he showed me on paper how our hunt should go. He had decided how long, in hours, it would take for us to get a caribou, a bear, and a moose, and in which order we should shoot them. He had figured how long we should take to get to camp, and how long it should take to move camp. He had the hunt laid out, in proper sequence, from beginning to end.

I listened to him, and commented, "You put me in mind of the efficiency expert, who, while he was reviewing workers in a factory, found a man with both hands and a foot busy. He looked him over for a while and says, 'We've got to find something for this guy to do with that other foot.'"

The man had never been on a guided hunt, yet he was telling me how to run my hunt.

"What are we supposed to do if we are hunting caribou, and find a good moose or bear trophy? If we shoot it, that would throw us way off of our schedule," I pointed out. "And then what would we do?"

He still couldn't see any reason why we shouldn't be able to work out more or less of a schedule. I kidded him along. "You

Slim Moore (right) and Phillip Neuweiler, a client from Pennyslvania, with a rather small caribou bull, 1962. Alaska Range. ROSEMARIE OLSEN

mean, we shouldn't shoot anything that comes along, no matter how good it looks, unless it's at the top of the list?

"My hunts are pretty hard to run on schedule," I gently explained. "But, we do the best we can, and have as good a time as possible. We might get her all done in three or four days, and we might hunt the full time and not get anything, but we always keep trying."

He decided to go along with that.

I hunted with the efficiency expert for about three weeks, and found him a caribou, a moose, and a bear. They weren't exactly on schedule, but I guess he adjusted his books so they fit in all right.

He must have been satisfied with the hunt, for I heard from him for the next two or three Christmases.

I've never been one to try to run a hunt on a rigid schedule. I might be hunting at four in the morning, and then be asleep on a sunny knoll in mid day.

Sometimes we have rough weather on a hunt. I once put in a full thirty day hunt without ever getting dry. What time there was for me to get my clothes dry, the hunters had so many wet clothes around the stoves that I decided to leave mine on. They dried eventually.

A COUPLE OF HUNTERS I ONCE GUIDED brought a photographer to take pictures of their hunt. He was a misfit. He could always find some excuse for not accompanying us when we left camp on day hunts. He had little understanding of hunting.

I found a bear eating on a caribou carcass, and the hunters wanted him to take pictures of them shooting it.

We tried to sneak up on the bear while it was feeding. The photographer, who was bear shy, rode a horse with a very tender mouth. We rode into little draw to keep out of the bear's sight. When we were about to leave the horses, to stop his horse he hauled back on the reins as hard as he could. The poor horse started to run backward and came to a little soft spot and sat on his rump and ended sitting, kind of like a dog.

The photographer slid off and started hollering and groaning, accusing the horse of bucking him off. I think he was scared that he couldn't outrun the bear we were trying to sneak up on.

When we finished counting his arms and legs, fingers, and toes and decided he was ok, we eased on foot to within 100 yards of the bear. It saw us and sloped. It had been alerted by the photographer's loud complaints. The hunters, who were upset, thinking the photographer was hurt, missed the bear and it got away. There were no pictures taken.

Next morning the photographer wanted someone to give him his breakfast in bed. He said he was pretty sure his leg was broken. When I looked at it, I couldn't see any difference between it and his other leg. There was no swelling or redness.

He continued the sham the following morning too, when it was a bit snowy—I figured the snowballs outside the warm tents were giving him problems, not his leg.

I usually guide small parties of one or two hunters, sometimes three. This was my biggest ever, with two hunters and their photographer, three guides (one for the photographer), a cook and a packer—eight men. For this crowd we had fourteen horses.

The hunters wanted to catch some fish before the hunt, which delayed our arrival in the high country where we hunted. Snow fell a week or ten days earlier than usual in the Alaska Range that year. It continued to fall through early September.

At the end of the hunt, around September 1, we had to cross 5,130-foot-high St. Anthony's Pass where there was two feet of wet snow. We had left a bunch of trophies and meat at Riley Creek, on the far side, and had to pick them up. I had stayed a little too long before tackling the pass. High passes in the Alaska Range aren't safe for travel generally after the first of September, and I knew it. I thought we'd be all right to and through September 1.

I was wrong.

As we headed for the pass, the weather and snow made the horses restless. We were out of feed for them, and we had to keep them hobbled. To add to our woes there weren't enough horses for the packs we had. The hunters and photographer rode, but some of the guides, including me, had to walk.

St. Anthony's pass is wide on top, with dangerous steep places on both sides (approaches) where, even without snow, it would be easy to roll a horse several hundred feet down a sheer wall. There are few places in that pass you can cross with horses. I pretty much knew the best route, and walked ahead of the outfit to find it.

Rock slides we climbed across were wet and slippery, and those of us who walked, and the horses, stumbled and slipped a lot. The summit is a big flat, but it has lots of small potholes that were snowed over. It was easy to step into one and fall down.

We labored through that pass for fourteen hellish hours. High Alaska Range mountain passes always have high winds. Not only was it cold, the wind almost blew riders out of the saddle. No one was dressed for that kind of weather. Those who rode were colder than those walking—we at least were getting a little exercise. Sometimes too much.

The photographer kept crowding his horse against me. I told him he if he really wanted to go any faster, I'd let him by. He backed off.

The wet snow balled up on the horse's feet, making them about a foot higher than they should have been. The hunters tended to get a little nervous and excited, and kept trying to rein their mounts. The animals needed to be left on their own and allowed to pick their way. It was not a pleasant time for man or horse.

When we reached the far side of the pass, and the last mile before our camp, I was so tired I thought I'd have to walk on my hands to get there. I was thinking there must be an easier way to make a living.

I RECEIVED A LETTER FROM TWO HUNTERS who wanted to book a brown bear hunt on the Alaska Peninsula. They wanted to bring John, a handicapped friend. He didn't get around very well walking, but he'd be ok on a horse, they wrote.

I told them there were no horses where I hunted on the Peninsula, but if they wanted to bring their friend, we'd do our best to accommodate him.

That was a mistake on my part, but I tried to live up to it.

I met the three in Anchorage, where John managed to get around on sidewalks, although he dragged one foot. When we arrived at Hoodoo Lake, in the vicinity of Port Moller, where I set up camp, I took him for a short walk. His foot hung up in the moss and brush. There was no way he could hike to get a bear.

"I'd sure like to get a bear," he told me. "I was razzed when I left home by some guys who said I wouldn't get one. I bet a pile of money I'd get a bear, and I'd like to collect."

That put me in an awkward position. I too would have almost bet that he wouldn't get a bear.

Over the next week or so, John lounged around camp sipping booze while his two friends hiked out with me and the other guide to kill nice trophy brownies.

With that accomplished, I told John I'd take him under my wing and see what we could do.

I had met a man who lived in that area who had a small plane. He occasionally flew to our camp to visit. We occasionally paid him to fly us groceries or other items we needed. I arranged for his adult grandson, who had a cabin boat, to take John and me to find a bear.

Arctic grayling are abundant and easily caught throughout Interior Alaska. They are white-fleshed and tasty. On light tackle they are good fighters. They will hit spoons, spinners, flies, or take baited hooks. Dry-fly fishing for grayling provides some of the most fun. JIM REARDEN

The man flew John and me to his home, and the grandson took us in his little boat along the Bering Sea coast, looking for a bear. We saw a big boar within an hour, close to the beach.

"I don't think I can get you close enough," the grandson said. I urged him to try. We were about a mile from the beach and it looked like good water to me. We started in and quickly went aground. The grandson knew what he was talking about.

He managed to back us off. He made a couple more attempts, and we finally ran ashore. The big boar was gone. Then we couldn't get off; the tide had dropped, and we had to spend twelve hours on a mud flat, with the boat out of water and dry, tipped almost on its side.

When the boat re-floated, we ran to Nelson Lagoon and up the Caribou River, stopping frequently to glass ahead for bears. No bears appeared. An old-timer who lived in the area offered to let us use a trapping cabin he owned on the Caribou.

When we reached the cabin, John was tired, it was late, and he decided to call it a day. The grandson said it was about as far upriver as we could go with the cabin boat anyway.

However, he had a skiff there with an outboard motor that we could use to run up river to a lake. After building a fire in the stove, we left John at the cabin, and we swiftly ran the eighteen miles to the lake.

John was from a southern state, and the ride to the lake in the skiff would probably have turned him to solid ice. At the lake I glassed around the edge and spotted a boar and a sow in a little patch of alders near the shoreline.

"Get us out of here without making any more noise," I urged the grandson.

John was in bed in rough shape when we arrived back at the cabin. He was an alcoholic, and was out of booze. He had had all kinds of things wrong with him while his friends had hunted —pleurisy, pneumonia, and one thing and another.

"We have a couple of bears tied up for you. If they don't break loose during the night, we might get a bear in the morning," I told him.

He didn't seem enthused over the trip in the open boat, but by next morning he felt better and we got an early start.

It was awfully cold as that swift boat ran up the Caribou River. I sat in the bow with John behind me, so he was somewhat sheltered from the wind.

When we reached the lake, where there had been two bears there were now four. They were about 150 yards inland from the beach.

I was in a quandary. Alaska's game regulations prohibit shooting big game from a motorized boat. The hunter was unable to walk. Should I break the law and allow him to shoot from the boat?

I solved the dilemma by telling the grandson, "Run your boat as fast as you can and hit that sandy beach with her wide open. Jerk your motor up just before we hit."

He did it perfectly. With the skiff run well up on the beach, I grabbed John and carried him about ten feet from the boat to where he could stand and see the bears.

The biggest of the four bears ran toward us. I thought for a moment he was going to charge, but he turned and ran to the lake and started to swim.

The next biggest bear stood on his hind legs, looking at us from about 150 yards.

"There's your bear. Take him before he runs," I shouted softly.

John had a fancy handmade .375 Magnum carbine. His shot literally swept that bear off his feet. It looked as if he had been hit by a giant hammer. John's bullet hit the bear's chest, missing the backbone.

The bear struggled to his feet, tottering. John then shot it in the neck to put it down for good. The other two bears ran.

I never saw anyone happier over getting a bear. To cap his joy, my friend with the airplane shortly arrived to check on us, landed, and flew John back to our main camp at Hoodoo Lake, where he had left his cache of booze.

When we got back to Anchorage, John spent about $250 on long distance calls to New York, Chicago, and elsewhere, bragging about the bear he had killed. I don't know how much he won in bets, but it must have been considerable.

THE FOLLOWING WASN'T FUNNY AT THE TIME, but I guess it was one of the funniest hunting experiences I've ever had. I saw the humor only afterward. It revolved around a cook I hired to accompany me on a hunt with two clients and another guide. Jake was recommended to me as a good cook. Perhaps he was. I don't know for sure.

Jake wore thick glasses; he couldn't see much without them. We were camped in woodstove-heated wall tents high in the Alaska Range. Camp was nicely set up, and the two clients and two guides (including me) hunted daily.

We soon learned that Jake was expecting an increase in his family. The event was to be announced over Fairbanks radio station KFAR, which had a popular evening program called Tundra Topics, in which messages were beamed to folks in the bush.

Jake had brought a small battery-powered radio, and he tuned it to KFAR at the appropriate time every evening. All of us gathered around in one of the tents to listen to that radio. As time went on, we became more and more interested, and, along with Jake, eager to hear the happy news. It became a major subject in camp.

When the announcement came, "It's a boy," everyone was in the tent.

Jake leaped up, ran out of the tent, and circled it, hollering, "It's a boy, it's a boy, it's a boy."

It apparently mattered not to Jake that there wasn't anyone else for miles around. We didn't have much time to wonder who he was hollering to, for he stumbled and fell flat across the tent ropes, and almost jerked the tent down. That pulled the stove pipe off of the wood stove, and the half-collapsed tent started filling with smoke.

Everyone bailed out of the smoke-filled tent, coughing, and we quickly retied the tent ropes. I went in and, with gloves on, put the stove pipe back in place.

That was the beginning.

During that high country hunt there were lots of young willow ptarmigan. I had brought shotguns, and the hunters enjoyed the wonderful wing shooting. The white wings and the noisy flushes of these two-pound birds is exciting. They were tender, berry-fat, and wonderful eating.

The day after the birth of Jake Jr., I arrived in camp early with one of the hunters and we ate an early dinner. I had instructed Jake to feed hunters and guides as soon as they arrived in camp from a day's hunt. My hunter for the day and I enjoyed a feed of fried ptarmigan, and we were sitting around visiting when the other guide and hunter arrived.

While they were washing up and getting ready to eat, Jake started to set a big platter of cooked ptarmigan on the table for them. The platter barely hit the table, and he dumped the whole works on the dirt floor.

He didn't think anyone was watching, and he swiftly picked 'em all up and stuck them back on the platter.

The hunter and I didn't say a word, but sat wondering how the other two fellows would react.

As he started to gnaw on a bird, the hunter asked, "Are you sure, Doc, when you cleaned these birds, that you didn't drop them in the sand? I seem to be getting sand in my teeth."

Doc says, "Hell no, I didn't drop no birds in the sand. But I'm also getting sand in my teeth. I don't know where it came from."

The other hunter and I sat there almost busting, but we didn't say a word. I was afraid to look at him, and he, likewise, was afraid to look at me. We'd have both roared. We were afraid they might hang Jake from one of the knotty spruce near camp.

I almost had to sit on my hands to keep from twisting Jake's neck.

Later, we moved the hunt to the Circle country along the Steese Highway north of Fairbanks to take some caribou, and to get some caribou photos. I took one of the hunters to mile-and-a-half by two-mile Medicine Lake. We didn't see any trophy-size moose, but we saw several little mulligan bulls.

That night in camp we talked about the mulligan bulls. Next morning, I noticed Jake called us to breakfast a little earlier than usual. One of the hunters with his guide planned to hunt around Medicine Lake, thinking they might take one of the little bulls.

Jake disappeared after breakfast, but I didn't think anything about it until later. The hunter and guide headed for Medicine Lake, and were nearly there when they heard a couple of shots. When they arrived at the lake, they found Jake there with a little mulligan bull moose he had shot. It lay in about eighteen-inches of water near the shoreline.

A local Native had left a canvas ratting canoe on the lakeshore —a tippy canvas over a kayak-like frame. Jake had paddled it out to the moose, tied a rope to the antlers, and was trying to tow the moose ashore. As the guide and hunter watched, Jake paddled as hard as he could on one side, then the other. The moose didn't move an inch.

"He's an idiot," the guide later commented.

Jake had no business sneaking off and shooting game on that hunt. The guide and hunter rescued him by helping him pull the moose ashore, more to prevent waste of meat, than to help Jake.

No experienced hunter ever kills a moose while it is standing in water – an entire moose is almost impossible to move to dry land, and it's a mess to dress while in the water. Meat, with water on it, is almost certain to spoil if it doesn't receive special care.

By then, we were all totally disgusted with Jake. When we broke camp we abandoned him and his moose there near Circle.

One of the clients returned the next year to hunt with me. He asked me to find another cook for the hunt.

SHEEP, CARIBOU, MOOSE, AND VARIOUS BIRDS can all be plucked clean of hair or feathers quickly and easily if you do it immediately after they hit the ground. Inexperienced guides occasionally ruin a cape (needed for a head mount) of a big game animal by starting to remove a cape too soon. Hair accidently removed by working on a cape too soon cannot be replaced.

Best cut a few willows, light a pipe, talk about the stalk or the hunter's marvelous shot, sharpen a knife, light a fire, clear some willows around the carcass—do anything that can take ten or fifteen minutes. Even then, test by pulling at hairs on a part of the body away from the cape to be sure the hair has set before starting to remove the cape.

With sheep and caribou, which have white hairs on head and neck, the prudent guide pulls the head uphill so blood from wounds or from gutting can't stain white neck and head hair.

If white hairs become bloodstained, water is usually near. Cold water will remove fresh blood stains. Once blood sets, water is little help. Then the stain is a problem for the taxidermist.

THE GUIDING BUSINESS can be precarious. You might have a dozen good hunts, and perhaps with no fault of yours, or even if it is your fault, you have one bad hunt. Weather might ruin a hunt. Game might be unusually scarce. Perhaps you have a couple of hunters who are impossible to please, no matter how hard you try.

That can hurt your reputation more than a good hunt helps it.

I've always done my best to please. I try to plan hunts so my clients can kill their trophies as quickly as possible, with the least risk to the hunter.

When I used horses for my hunts, I generally made a trip into the area I planned to hunt to pack in staples – things bears and other critters wouldn't bother—and checked out the game situation.

Game animals move about; one year they might be abundant in an area. A year later they may be abundant twenty miles from there.

I started about thirty days before a hunt, shoeing horses and getting equipment together and seeing it was in top shape. I often put out caches of supplies in and near the area I planned to hunt.

I also worked the kinks out of my horses. Often they hadn't been worked for maybe a year, and I'd see to it that they didn't have much bucking in them. I'd take a string out and tail them on the trail (tie horses to each other by their tail) so they'd learn to follow a trail and not spread out all over the country. This avoided having horses getting bogged down, and made life a lot easier during a hunt.

Even today, when we depend on airplanes or crawler vehicles to get to hunting areas, a guide should know the game situation before taking hunters to it.

I always try to have a comfortable tent camp set up and everything ready when my hunters arrive.

I never used cots when I used horses—they're heavy and bulky. I used air mattresses and most of the time camped in timber where I could be generous with spruce feathers, even with the air mattresses.

I make a point not to use the same camp sites year after year. It is just as easy to pick one a few hundred yards away where there is no sign of wood cutting. It would be nice and convenient to have permanent camps all over your hunting country, but a lot of hunters would think they were in an area that was hunted out.

Camp robbers (northern jay, or gray jay) a long-tailed, eleven-inch-long jay found commonly in Alaska's Interior, can be a serious pest in a hunting camp. They love meat, and can do an amazing amount of damage to moose, sheep, or caribou meat hanging in camp. They always seem to know the choicest parts. They'll steal, eat, or soil other exposed food, too.

Years ago I talked with Andy Taylor, a great mountain climber, about putting out caches of food. He had a lot of experience leaving food on mountains where there was nothing but rocks. Camp robbers commonly follow people around, and they'll even find food caches well above timberline and on mountain sides.

Taylor told me. "Put a tarp down, put your food on it, and another tarp over the top, weighed down with rocks. Then pour a stream of cayenne pepper around it."

I've since built a lot of caches in the hills. Sometimes on a big hunt I take a lot of grub and cache it here and there. Sometimes I take as much as two pounds of cayenne pepper, which is a whole lot. I've had some cooks about ready to walk off when they found it, so I have to be careful to warn them.

Camp robbers like to sit on and peck at hanging meat, and somehow they seem to select the best, like the rounds and loins. I've learned to let one or two get a couple of feeds so there would be a hole or two in the meat where they have fed. Then I heap cayenne in those holes, knowing they'll go back to where they've already fed.

They'll come back and take a bite or two, then fly up a nearby tree and holler and scream. They shake their bill, sneeze, and make an awful commotion. They'll fly around and and holler. Treat one that way, and his reaction tells the others the story, and it keeps them all away from the meat. They have a language of their own, and pass the word when they get a bait of cayenne. It's probably a good thing I don't understand what they are saying.

The stuff keeps flies off, too, and it works with parka (ground) squirrels. These little gray burrowing squirrels like to dig into a tent or a cabin and they can cause a lot of damage. I sprinkle it in holes and cracks and around the edges of a tent or cabin, and it keeps them out. The secret is, be generous with the stuff. Then it works.

MAJOR HOPKINS, who was nearly 70, was my client for a hunt along in the mid-1930s. He was an awfully nice fellow. I found him a nice Dall ram, a good bull caribou, and a fine moose. However, he was bent on getting a grizzly bear; I think he wanted a bear more than any of the others.

That year there were very few salmon in Alaska Range streams where I hunted, and the bears, instead of being concentrated around salmon streams and lakes, were scattered all over looking for food.

I took the Major to a lake where normally there are spawning salmon in September. We were lucky. While walking around the shoreline, in the distance we spotted a fine big bear that was also walking around the lake. He was heading our way.

It was well into September, and the bear, which had a beautiful unusual-colored silvery coat, kept poking into the lake looking for salmon. Hopkins excitedly stared at him with his binoculars.

We got under cover to wait for the bear to come to us. The big bruiser waded about, peering into the water, searching for the salmon that normally would have been spawning along the lake edge.

It was evident that he couldn't find any. He finally gave up and took to the hills. We tried to cut him off. We had good cover, and occasionally we got a good look at him. He worked berry patches that were maybe 100 feet square—but it was a year in which berries were about as scarce as salmon. He cleaned this patch and that, moving swiftly from one to the other.

As we chased that bear, the Major soon became winded, and we weren't gaining on the bear. It took some time for us to get within about 400 yards. I tried getting more speed out of him in vain. We were always in the open when the bear fed and we had to remain still. When the bear moved, we did too. Finally we were within

200 yards, and I saw it was going to be our last chance. Sadly, my hunter didn't have the extra burst of energy to get closer.

"You'd better shoot from here," I told him.

He lay prone, and even then I could see his rifle barrel moving from his heavy breathing. The poor man gasped for breath as he tried to hold his scope on the bear.

His shot hit low. It was close enough to knock moss and other stuff on the bear. The bear whirled and ran. The Major got in one more shot, which also missed. Griz soon dropped over a steep embankment and out of sight. The next time we saw him he was a quarter of a mile away, still steaming away at full speed.

We hunted bears for about a week of the forty days we were out, and I never did get him close enough, and in condition, to shoot, a bear.

Hopkins was an awful crank on fish. He had written a book on the fish or North America. I think he preferred fishing to hunting, which, to me, made him a bit odd. He chose to alternate between fishing and hunting; three or four days for each.

I turned his gray hair a little grayer when we fished. "Don't ever leave Alaska to fish, Slim. You'll never be able to catch fish anywhere else in the world," he told me.

When I fished next to him, he accused me of making my line whistle, and my flies pop. He soon undertook to make a fisherman out of me. After a time, I told him I should be paying him instead of him paying me.

We went to the Gulkana River where the grayling were so thick they'd hit any kind of a fly or lure. He got a tremendous kick out of that – as much a thrill, I think, as he got out of the three good trophies he shot. He must have caught and released hundreds of grayling, all with barbless flies he had tied.

He even had me fishing with a book under my arm so I would use my arm from elbow to wrist.

"You look like you're chopping wood, Slim," he scolded, as I cast. "That's no way to fish. You really shouldn't treat fish that way; they deserve more respect," he told me.

He had spent much time in England, and told me how particular and careful they were there about tying flies to fit the rise of fish in a river.

I told him I doubted I'd ever get that good, that I thought I'd stay with the country fish in Alaska – fish that didn't know any better. "Besides," I said, "I figured that all the smart animals crawled out of the water long ago."

The good Major was disappointed in that he didn't get a grizzly, and so was I. It was an awful letdown for both of us when he failed to get that silver-coated grizzly.

13. Stalking Sheep, and Memories of Early Days

ON ONE OF MY FIRST HUNTS with Fred Hollander, he was a bit suspicious that a hunt wouldn't be as good as I claimed it would be. He suggested I should first go alone to see if there were any sheep in the area where I proposed taking him.

"Don't worry, there are plenty of sheep there," I assured him.

I got a little pack string together and we headed to Morningstar Creek in the Granite Range. We traveled as far up as there were willows in the bottom of the creek. We could see sheep on both sides. As we rode along in the creek bottom, only our heads were visible to the sheep. They ran. No Alaska big game animal has sharper eyes than Dall sheep.

We followed the creek up until we were at about the same level as most of the sheep. "There must have been a lot of hunting here for sheep to be that wild," Hollander commented.

"There hasn't been any hunting here this year," I told him.

We had just checked my camp of the previous year, and everything was the way I had left it. I knew if hunters had been here, they'd have used my camp.

"I've never seen sheep so wild. Those sheep are a quarter of a mile away, and they're still running," he cranked.

When the sheep were at about 300 yards, where they felt safe, they stopped. We reached the head of the draw, tied the horses, and walked into plain sight of the sheep.

"I think I can kill one from here," Hollender said. He was excited. He was also an excellent shot. He always carried a jointed alpine stick, steel-shod on the bottom, and split up the center, with a bolt across the top. Whenever he shot, he rested his rifle on this bolt.

I wanted him closer, for a more certain shot.

Sheep were all around us, now including about twenty rams.

"Let's walk a little way towards those rams," I suggested, starting off.

He was reluctant. "I can't hit anything that's running," he claimed. I ignored him, and kept walking. It was our first day afield for that season, and I needed to get a little control.

He joined me, lagging a bit. We walked slowly in plain sight toward the sheep. They could now see more than just our heads. The rams allowed us to walk to within about 150 yards before they became nervous.

When hunting sheep, I try to keep out of sight as much as possible. Sometimes, if they see just a little of you, they become suspicious and may flee, perhaps thinking wolf or coyote—as they did when they saw our heads as we rode up the creek bed. Sheep are more alert to danger from below, than to anything that might arrive from the mountains above.

If they see your entire body in plain sight, they may be curious enough to stand and watch, and allow you to move within easy range, as they did for us that day.

"This is too much," he said. "I'm going to shoot one from here."

He jerked his alpine stick apart, sat down, rested his rifle on it, and shot a big ram. It was as simple as that.

While I dressed the ram, the other sheep eased to within seventy-five yards of us. There they stood staring, apparently curious.

Hollender took photos of the peering sheep while I worked on the downed ram.

"I'm amazed," he finally said. "I thought they'd bolt when we walked toward them like that."

Caribou also will often allow you to walk toward them, provided the wind is in your favor. If a caribou gets antsy, lie down where he can hardly see you, and often he'll get inquisitive. I've had them swim lakes and come to look me over. They circle at a

August Sunstedt, with a Dall ram taken while hunting with Slim Moore fifteen miles back from the face of Castner Glacier, Alaska Range. 1928. CREDIT ROSEMARIE OLSEN

high trot until they get your wind, then they'll go straight up in the air, come down in the same spot, and take off.

On one occasion one of my hunters and I were at Ober Creek, and saw a nice caribou bull out in the open. We were skylined on a gravel ridge, and so was the bull when he raised his head and peered at us. It was the first day of the hunt, and we didn't care whether we killed a caribou that day.

When we went prone, that bull went down a draw, and we kind of forgot about him. It was a sunny day, and we were relaxed and moving easy. Suddenly, he popped up about fifty yards from us. He started to circle, to pick up our wind. This gave us a good chance to look him over carefully. He looked like a real trophy, so the hunter shot him.

That bull traveled 450 or 500 yards to look us over.

Hollender and I spent a week there at Morningstar, mostly taking pictures of the sheep. On our last day Hollender selected and shot another big ram.

At the end of our hunt, Hollender admitted, "This is most sheep and the best sheep country I've ever seen."

We returned to Morningstar the following year, hoping to collect a record ram, but we were snowed out. My horses were accustomed to wintering only twenty-five miles from there, and I had to keep them hobbled to prevent them from taking off for their winter range.

We were short of horse feed, and there was snow on the ground. If I took hobbles off so they could feed, they'd run off; if I left hobbles on, they couldn't feed.

We stuck it out for two days, and the snow continued to pile up, so we had to pull out. Leaving the horses, we crossed the Delta River and hunted the mountains next to Black Rapids Glacier where Hollender killed a nice ram, although it wasn't a record.

⁌

WHEN THE ALASKA RAILROAD was completed in 1923, frozen or chilled meat could be shipped from Seattle to Alaska's interior. Prior to that, moose, caribou, and Dall sheep killed by market hunters was the primary source of meat for Fairbanksans and other nearby non-bush populations.

Tender, mild, and flavorful Dall sheep meat was the favorite of most residents, and still is for those who are familiar with Alaska's big game meats.

Market hunters operated in virtually all main drainages on the north side of the Alaska Range within dog-team-freighting distance of Fairbanks. In 1917 a Fairbanks warden estimated that, during the previous four years, 2,800 Dall sheep had been killed for the market within 200 miles of Fairbanks.

A favorite Dall sheep hunting ground for market hunters was the sheep licks on Dry Creek, about eighty miles southeast of Fairbanks in the foothills of the Alaska Range. Here sheep have licked at the salty earth so long they can walk out of sight into the depressions the licking has created. It's easy to reach by dog team, and for many years tons of sheep meat left there on dog sleds bound for Fairbanks.

I went to Dry Creek for the first time in the early 1930s, five years after market hunting had effectively ended. A violent four-day storm kept the sheep away, but when it ended, they arrived in almost unbelievable numbers. I climbed a hill where I could watch, and it was like being on an Idaho sheep ranch. At times 400 or more sheep were within sight. Sheep trotted across the hills behind the lick as far as I could see. Alaska Range Dalls have not been that abundant since the 1930s.

They arrived in little bunches and eagerly ran into the lick, which, to them, must taste like ice cream. They also ran from the lick, for they were vulnerable to wolves or coyotes while crowded together against the worn, cave-like licks.

Near the licks I saw, scattered on the ground, leftovers of market hunting—what would have made a full bushel of brass cartridge cases of about every caliber of rifle made. They hadn't deteriorated noticeably, except that most had turned black.

German-born Hugo Stromberger settled at the Dry Creek sheep lick in 1922. He could sit in one of his cabins and through a window watch sheep coming to the lick. He trapped marten, fox, wolves, and wolverine during winter, and in spring, summer, and fall he shot sheep and an occasional moose and caribou for the market. He also illegally fed sheep, moose, and caribou meat to his sled dogs.

He continued to shoot and market sheep meat for many years after 1925 when a law ended the practice. That ended in November, 1939, when Alaska Game Commission Wardens Sam O. White and Wayne House caught him with fifty-one illegally killed Dall sheep, two illegally killed cow moose, and two illegally killed caribou. In addition he had three set guns (guns set to fire at intruders when doors were opened at his cabins). Set guns were not popular in a thinly settled land where hospitality is a normal way of life.

Stromberger was sentenced to six months in jail, and fined $150.

THERE IS FAR MORE TO HUNTING than the killing. Seeing wildlife, sensing the mood of a wilderness, knowing the nearest other humans may be twenty-five or fifty miles away, feeling the cozy warmth of a woodstove-heated tent after a long day of hunting, companionship with others who enjoy the wilds—all of these things and more make up the complexities of a satisfying hunt. These are the goals I set for the hunts I have always tried to provide my clients.

One of the regrets I have about the guiding business in Alaska is the change from the past. From the 1920s into the 1950s, a normal hunt lasted thirty to forty-five days. In recent years, hunters expect to bag trophies in ten days what they used to take in thirty days.

A hunt with horses used to be a leisurely, enjoyable time. It was easy to move camp, fun to camp in new places, and challenging to seek the best possible trophies for hunters. With horses we could reach hunting grounds where even an airplane can't land today

The airplane has changed guided hunts in Alaska. Now a plane lands hunters, guides, and camp gear usually at a lake, and they are stuck there until the plane comes back, unless they engage the plane for the full time of the hunt. Few hunters are willing to pay for this service.

Even with a plane supporting you full time, you hunt entirely on foot, which is different from being able to climb on a horse to let him climb the hills for you.

When you depend on an airplane for transportation, bad weather can pin you to a camp area indefinitely. With horses, you can tackle tough weather if you really want to hunt or move camp.

Hunters commonly expect to hunt in bad weather nowadays, because their hunts are so short. On my horse hunts, when fog settled and hid the mountains, wind howled, or heavy rain poured, hunters enjoyed relaxing in warm and dry tents, played cards,

Slim's pack string, going to Riley Creek for a hunt, in the Alaska Range, 1930. L R Howard Hooper, Slim Moore, Doc Hufman, Doc Carter, Eggleson. ROSEMARIE OLSEN

read, or visited, while peering out to watch for nearby wildlife and possible trophies. There was plenty of time to hunt.

A hunt I made in 1941, before World War II, is a good example. In the spring of that year I received a letter from a Kansas doctor who had obtained my name from one of his patients. He was 75 years old, and had just retired. He had long dreamed about hunting and fishing in Alaska, and would like to spend a month or more with me on a guided hunt.

He told me he had a wonky heart, but controlled it with medication. He thought he could handle hunting on horseback, so long as the days didn't get too long.

He ended his letter by saying, "I don't have many years left. Though I haven't hunted, or even fished very much, I've long dreamed of a guided hunt into the wilds of Alaska. Can you help me?"

My partner guide for that forty-five-day hunt with the doctor was George Bishop, who, during the World War II, was a member of Castner's Cutthroats (the famed Alaska Scouts) who served heroically in the Aleutian Campaign to help drive the Japs from Alaska.

The doctor decided he'd like to fish for the first few days of our hunt. With three saddle horses and four pack horses, we went to the Tangle Lakes, a cluster of big, deep, clear lakes alive with grayling and lake trout. [Today, the Denali Highway, completed in 1957, passes next to these lakes.]

We took the good doctor to a spring that was loaded with four or five layers of grayling, with perhaps 500 of them in an area you could easily cover with a fly rod or a casting rod.

The doctor's inexperience was against him. The grayling leaped at his flies all right, but he couldn't seem to hook them.

"We'll have to take you where the fishing is a little better," I promised. Bishop and I took him to a little fast-flowing channel that ran between lakes. I tied a little Colorado spinner to his line, and told him to have at it. I knew the current would hook the fish.

For about an hour, I sat on the bank and reached out and unhooked and released foot-long grayling as he caught them. After about an hour he said, "Let's go up the stream. I'm tired of catching the same fish all the time."

He thought he was catching one fish over and over; he was unaware that grayling schools are often all of one size.

Fishing was so good that it was no good. The doctor finally understood that, and he had a wonderful time moving about and catching and releasing grayling, many of which were more than a foot long. In the three days we fished at Tangle Lakes, he caught and released several hundred of these brightly-colored, flag-waving, fighters, plus a dozen or so lake trout, one of which weighed twenty pounds.

We then rode the horses into the Jarvis Creek country, and crossed through 5,130-foot St. Anthony Pass. Shortly after we left the pass the doctor slumped from his saddle and fell to the ground, unconscious.

He had told me he carried his nitroglycerin tablets in his shirt pocket. I found them, slipped one under his tongue, and vigorously fanned him with my hat, fervently hoping he would snap out of it.

He came to shortly and smiled, saying, "Sorry about that. Thanks for giving me that tablet. I'll be ok in a bit."

He was, although he remained wobbly for a couple hours.

I was thankful I had put him on a gentle horse, and that he

had fallen in a soft spot; I worried he would pass out again and hit his head on a rock.

He did pass out several more times while riding. Luckily, he fell in a soft spot each time. I suspect the high altitude and low oxygen had something to do with it. At the end of the hunt, I told him he owed me a new hat because I almost wore my old one out fanning him.

I knew of a high ridge, where one side was easily climbed by horses, and the far side was rocky and rough where rams often hung out. The doctor, George, and I rode to the ridge top where George stayed with the horses and the doctor and I slipped a short way down the rough side, looking for rams.

We found three widely scattered as they fed across a steep hillside. One, which had full curl horns, was about 150 yards below us.

For a couple of weeks I had helped the doctor to get familiar with his new .30-06 rifle with daily target practice, and he had become fairly consistent at hitting a target.

"Pretend there's a target on that ram; hold just behind the front leg and squeeze the trigger. Take your time," I instructed.

He did as I asked. At his shot the ram dropped and stayed down. It was the first big game animal he had ever shot.

From one of our camps in a grove of big spruce trees, with binoculars we watched as an occasional caribou moved across a large flat. One early morning George, the doctor, and I rode to the middle of the flat and climbed a small knob. Most of the caribou we had seen had fed around it. Caribou, of course, feed and move constantly.

We tied the horses, and sat atop that knob. It was a pleasant, warm September day, and with glasses we enjoyed seeing the occasional caribou pass by. Each fed in the usual caribou bite-here-and-bite-there manner, as they passed by. Most were cows, some with calves, but a few were young bulls just shedding their antlers' velvet.

We ate lunch, snoozed, and enjoyed the warm sun as we watched the wildlife around us. Sheep were slowly moving white dots high on nearby ridges. A sow grizzly with two cubs fed on berries on the flat where the caribou traveled. The cubs wrestled and chased, and once nursed, as we watched. The doctor was entranced by all of this.

Late in the day George, peering through his binocular, said, "I think I see what we've come here for."

The doc and I, with glasses, looked where George pointed, to see the snowy white neck of a mature caribou bull as it slowly worked our way. As it neared, we studied it with a spotting scope. It carried rocking-chair-size bright yellow antlers. As he fed, those antlers bobbed and flashed in the sun with every bite.

"Here comes your trophy caribou," I told the doc.

He peered through the scope, and looked at me wide-eyed. "Do you think we could get him?" he asked.

Every caribou we had seen had followed about the same route past our lookout knob, and every one had come within range. I was fairly sure the big bull would follow the same route.

"You can count on it, Doc," I assured him.

An hour or so later, as the lowering sun neared the top of the nearby mountains, the bull was within 200 yards. Then he was within 150 yards, and the good doctor, from a prone position, dropped him with one shot.

I have a vivid memory of one of our Alaska Range camps we used while on that hunt. The nearest humans were perhaps fifty miles distant. While in that camp, we neither saw nor heard any airplanes.

Our woodstove-heated wall tents were pitched in a beautiful stand of tall spruces, and the scent of those trees filled the air. An ice-cold, gin clear, little river flowed near. We had fly rods leaning against handy trees, and whenever one of us felt the urge, we could catch (and release) grayling with about every other cast.

There was plenty of dry wood for our stoves. The tents faced a green meadow where my horses fed, and above it was a snow-covered peak of the Alaska Range. Between us and that peak were several high ridges across which were scattered moving white Dall sheep.

I set a spotting scope up on a tripod, with which we could watch the sheep, an occasional grizzly on the sheep ridges, and moose in the valley where we were camped.

One day while in that camp, George spotted a great bull moose with big-palmed, many-pointed antlers that spread a full sixty inches. He was only a quarter of a mile away. He and the doctor slipped through the timber and sneaked to within fifty yards of him. The

Chief cook and bottle washer—Slim officiating as cook. Note perfect condition of the white tea kettle. Slim kept his camp equipment in new shape. No old beat-up junk in his camp. Rosemarie Olsen

Doc's first shot, in the rut-swollen neck, knocked the bull down, but he got up. His second shot, in the chest, stopped him for good.

At that point in the hunt the good doctor was walking on air.

The weather blessed us while we were there. Mornings were crisp and cold. Days were mostly clear with plenty of warmth from the sun. Nights we enjoyed the wood-stove-heated tents and lantern-light suppers. We had enough leisure to bake bread. We make hotcakes mornings, and often accompanied them with sheep, moose, or caribou steaks.

We yarned most nights, enjoying a few drinks as we sat around a campfire until the chill of evening sent us to our sleeping bags. One evening as we sat yarning, a wolf on a nearby ridge howled for nearly half an hour. A full moon filled the sky that night. Perhaps the wolf was howling at it. All three of us remembered that evening as something special.

It was an Eden. After the war, George Bishop told me that while he fought the Japs in the Aleutians, he often thought about that camp, and resolved, if he survived the war, to return to that site to see if it was as wonderful as he remembered.

After taking sheep, caribou, and moose in the Alaska Range, the three of us hunted brown bears on Hinchenbrook and Montague Islands in Prince William Sound. To finish the forty-five days, we hunted ducks and geese on the Copper River flats.

We never hurried. We had a comfortable camp every night. The doctor took a lot of pictures, saw a lot of wildlife, collected some fine trophies, and enjoyed a variety of Alaska's wilderness. He left, happy and satisfied.

His life's dream had come true.

That is the way to hunt and enjoy Alaska. Sadly, such leisurely hunts are mostly of the past.

THIS VOLUME COVERS THE HUNTING ADVENTURES, and wilderness wisdom, of Slim Moore's first thirty years (1926–56) in Alaska. He continued to work as a hunting guide for another twenty-three years. In the early 1960s, he sold Summit Lake Lodge to Dave Lanni, who was a former Protection Officer (Game Warden) for the Alaska Department of Fish and Game.

After selling the lodge, Slim and his wife Margaret moved to Anchorage. He continued to work as a hunting guide until 1979. When he retired at the age of 80, Moore was the oldest active licensed big game guide in Alaska.

Also by Jim Rearden

Hunting Alaska's Far Places
Half a Century with Rifle and Shotgun

Sam O. White, Alaskan
Tales of a Legendary Wildlife Agent and Bush Pilot

Forgotten Warriors of the Aleutian Campaign

Alaska's Wolf Man
The 1915–55 Wilderness Adventures of Frank Glaser

The Wolves of Alaska
A Fact-based Saga

Castner's Cutthroats
Saga of the Alaska Scouts

Koga's Zero
The Fighter that Changed World War II

Travel Air NC9084
The History of a 75-year-old Working Airplane

Jim Rearden's Alaska
Fifty Years of Frontier Adventure

All books in this list of twelve can be found in most Alaska's book stores. The above nine books may also be ordered directly from the publisher (406) 549-8488. See copyright page for address, website, e-mail, and fax number.

Arctic Bush Pilot
From Navy Combat to Flying Alaska's Northern Wilderness

Tales of Alaska's Big Bears

Shadows on the Koyukuk
An Alaskan Native's Life Along the River